Just Married, Please Excuse

Yashodhara Lal is a marketing professional with over twelve years of experience in the corporate world. She is also a trained dance-fitness instructor and yoga enthusiast.

She lives in Gurgaon with her husband Vijay and their three children nicknamed Peanut, Pickle and Papad. She writes about her family and her books on her entertaining blog at www.yashodharalal.com. You can also find her on Facebook.com/Yashodharalal or Twitter.com/yashodharalal.

Just Married, Please Excuse is Yashodhara's first book. Her second book, *Sorting Out Sid*, was published in 2014. Her third novel, *Dear Rimi*, is going to be out in 2015 and she is currently working on her fourth.

Just Married, Please Excuse

Yashodhara Lal

HarperCollins *Publishers* India

First published in India in 2012 by
HarperCollins *Publishers* India

Copyright © Yashodhara Lal 2012, 2013

P-ISBN: 978-93-5029-227-3
E-ISBN:978-93-5029-960-9

2 4 6 8 10 9 7 5 3

Yashodhara Lal asserts the moral right
to be identified as the author of this work.

HarperCollins *Publishers*
A-75, Sector 57, Noida, Uttar Pradesh 201301, India
77-85 Fulham Palace Road, London W6 8JB, United Kingdom
Hazelton Lanes, 55 Avenue Road, Suite 2900, Toronto, Ontario M5R 3L2
and 1995 Markham Road, Scarborough, Ontario M1B 5M8, Canada
25 Ryde Road, Pymble, Sydney, NSW 2073, Australia
10 East 53rd Street, New York NY 10022, USA

Typeset in Adobe Garamond 11.5/14
Jojy Philip, New Delhi 110 015

Printed and bound at
Thomson Press (India) Ltd.

To my family – for the material they provide

PART I

CAUTION

MARRIAGE

AHEAD

1

Pop Goes the Question

'Achha, I've been meaning to ask you,' Vijay said casually over the phone. 'When do you think we should get married?'

The question caught me off guard since the only build up to it had been our wishing each other a rather soppy, lovey-dovey good morning. I paused for a moment to give it a considered response.

'Eh?'

I was never at my eloquent best when taken by surprise.

I looked at my phone with raised eyebrows as though Vijay could see my questioning expression. Considering that we had been seeing each other for only three months and that I was in my early twenties and just out of management college, I was completely unprepared for even the mention of marriage. But here it was – an unmistakable, undeniable, definite mention.

'Married?' I choked out the words with some difficulty. 'Ha ha! You're joking, right? I'm only twenty-three – a mere *child*. You want to be held directly responsible for child marriage? No, na?'

I heard a by-now familiar stifled sigh at the other end of the line. 'Honey, mujhe pata hain you're twenty-three. But I'm thirty and I can only hold my parents off for so long. You know they're starting to look for arranged marriage matches for me. Again.'

I did know this and didn't particularly like it. I became petulant. 'So tell them to butt out. Or *maybe*,' I added spitefully, 'you should just go and marry some Harbinder or Buntvinder that they choose for you.'

'Buntvinder?' he chuckled. 'That's not even a real name. But tumhare liye achha hain, actually – my little Buntvinder. Ha ha.'

He sensed I was not amused and his voice became serious again. 'Look, we are eventually getting married, right? So why not now?'

'Vijay! We've only been going out for three months …'

'Arrey! I'm old-fashioned … I don't understand all this going-out, shoing-out stuff. I thought you were as serious about it as I am.'

'Of course I am as serious about it as you are. I just didn't know that you were so … serious!'

This time, his sigh was not as stifled as the previous one. 'Okay then. I guess we'll talk about it some other time. See you in the evening.'

Exchanging goodbyes that were a little colder than usual, we hung up and I flopped my head back onto my pillow. I was definitely *not* prepared for a discussion like this. Besides, it was one of those beautiful chilly Saturday mornings in Bangalore which are best spent lazing in bed. So although it was already 9 a.m., I had still been in the process of waking up when Vijay called. He, on the other hand, had taken the early morning flight for a day-trip to Delhi and had already been up for about five hours before he called me. He thus had the unfair advantage of a fresh and alert mind.

I realized that I wasn't going to be able to sleep now anyway and thought I might as well make some sort of an attempt to get out of bed. I looked around the sparse room of the company guest house in which I was staying and decided it wasn't even worth trying to get the so-called caretaker to make me a nice refreshing cup of tea. That dude was even grumpier than I was in the mornings. Despite the severe handicap of no tea, I bravely managed to push myself out of bed and spread my arms wide and yawned, indulging in a long, slow stretch. It looked like it would be an empty sort of day – a Saturday without Vijay was no fun.

Yeah, but still … twenty-three, I reminded myself, was just too young to get married.

I briefly considered telling myself that perhaps I was actually very mature for my age, but then rejected that on the grounds that it was a blatant lie. I definitely wasn't ready.

How did you *know* you were ready, anyway?

In any case, I wasn't altogether convinced I was the marrying type at all. I'd always liked to think of myself as a bit of a wild, free spirit. And right now, I had most of that beautiful decade – my twenties – ahead of me. Full of possibilities for adventure, exploration, thrills and – who knew, I thought a bit fancifully, maybe even a spot of danger. All this, notwithstanding the fact that I had just finished my MBA and entered the corporate world, as an employee in a large, staid MNC. Still. There could be *some* form of danger while peddling soaps and detergents.

But the only danger now seemed to be of getting trapped in a domestic rut and becoming a house-minding, wifely Buntvinder myself. The self-image that this conjured up in my mind inspired me to immediately start the day with a workout. And so I lay down and began to practise some contortions I had seen on the Yoga DVD I had obtained about a month ago from my mother. Even while I struggled to breathe correctly – or rather, to just breathe – during the dhanurasana, sarvangasana and other assorted asanas, I couldn't get our conversation out of my mind.

I knew that Vijay's parents had heard nothing of my existence. They had been pressurizing him to get married for a while now and had been lining up 'meetings' with nice girls from respectable families all over the country, but mostly from his hometown of Jaipur. 'At least just meet her' was their constant refrain. To oblige them, sometimes he did.

I had discovered that even before I had come into his life a few months ago, Vijay had found his own unique, rather intriguing way of getting his parents to ease up on the topic, if only temporarily.

He would simply get himself rejected.

It was quite a feat for him to get rejected – tall, good-looking, IIT-Delhi graduate from respectable brahmin family, working in a large MNC and all that jazz. Still, he manfully rose to the task and achieved it through the simple means of being obnoxious.

During each of these meetings, there would inevitably come a point when he and the girl were left alone to get to know each other better. He would act normal enough to begin with. Then, at some stage, he would clear his throat, look deep into her eyes and say in a low, serious voice, 'Look, Buntvinder (hypothetically speaking). Before we think about whether we should take things any further, there is something I have to ask you.'

She would lower her eyes and reply breathlessly, 'Go ahead.'

'It's something very deeply personal, and I'll understand if you don't want to answer it.'

'It's okay, you can ask me.'

'It's just that for me – and I hope for you – marriage

is not a thing to be taken lightly. So I really need to know this …'

She would be very nervous by now, but would steel herself in preparation for the worst. 'It's okay, Vijay! What is it you want to know?'

'I just need to know,' he would lower his voice even further and after a dramatic pause for effect, say, 'Who *was* the first Mughal emperor of India?'

The ensuing silence would only be broken by the sound of his loud guffaws at the look on her face. The responses ranged from huffy walk-outs to cushions thrown at his head. Either way, the girl would get the message that this wasn't a suitable boy, although the parents involved were never sure exactly why.

Being an easygoing and open-minded sort of chap, Vijay was not opposed to introducing a variation once in a while. As in the case of the overly sweet and sensitive young girl that he met in Jaipur, whom he didn't have the heart to try the usual Mughal emperor prank on.

Instead, after around twenty minutes of conversation – nervous and shy on her part, friendly and encouraging on his – he sidled up to her, making her back further into the sofa they were sitting on. He gazed into her eyes and murmured, 'You are one of the sweetest girls I have ever met in my life.' As she blushed in flustered confusion at this unexpected display of forwardness, he put his arm around her shoulders and whispered in her ear, 'And don't worry, I will *personally* find a nice boy for you.'

The poor girl was in tears by the time he left. Finally, his parents had eased up on the match-fixing efforts. Only temporarily, of course.

When I first saw Vijay in the office three months earlier, my first thought had been, 'Wow, that guy has *long* legs – where do they make pants his size?' He was a tall, lanky young man with smooth hair and a boyish-looking face that belied his thirty years.

I was only a lowly management trainee, fresh out of IIM-Bangalore, and Vijay had been in the organization for several years. We both worked in the marketing department, and had been introduced by his boss Madhukar, who also happened to be my project guide. I was impressed by Vijay from the beginning – that is, I thought he was cute. I liked him even more when I got to know him better and found that he was a laid-back, down-to-earth young man, with an extremely quirky sense of humour. He stood out in the corporate environment – literally, because at six foot two, he also towered over most other people.

The office campus was a beautiful one. It was built over a very large area of land on the outskirts of Bangalore, with plenty of greenery around. The building itself was a quaint old structure and from the outside was more reminiscent of an ancient castle than a modern office. You would enter through large ornate doors into a spacious lobby, upon the walls of which hung some great works of art – priceless pieces by M.F. Hussain and the like. There was even an impressive bronze statue of a raging bull, bang in the centre of the lobby. The fact that it faced away from the lobby entrance, and therefore you had a bull's backside greeting you every morning as you entered the office, did little to detract from the timeless charm of the building.

So, this was where we first met. Where our little romance started. Where we took our many after-lunch strolls around the campus. Where I once caught a glimpse of Vijay sitting at the large window of his ground-floor room, gazing outside in deep thought, immersed in what was probably some important business problem. I had watched him admiringly for a few moments, thinking how picturesque the scene was, and trying to come up with an appropriate title for it in my head, something like 'Long-legged Professional Contemplation'. Exactly at this point, the object of my scrutiny had coolly swung his legs over the sill and slipped out of the office in one smooth motion, presumably for a smoke. I was taken aback by his exiting in such a novel fashion and had thought for the first time – but certainly not the last, 'Man. That dude is weird.'

Later, I asked him out of curiosity what he thought when he first met me. He replied spontaneously – a bad habit he would soon learn to curb to some extent – 'I thought, Arrey yaar, here's yet another trainee to waste my time – but she's a rather cute jhalli.'

I didn't really know at the time what the term 'jhalli' meant, but I could sense it wasn't anything very complimentary. Vijay never offered compliments unless they were double-edged – part of his charm, I supposed.

He had done his share of stretching the truth to try and impress me. When he learnt that I was into music and playing the guitar, he said casually, 'Oh really? You know, I played the drums in college.'

This greatly raised him in my esteem. It was only later that I discovered that he had been referring to *one* specific occasion ten years ago when he had happened to pass by the auditorium, seen the IIT rock band members taking a break during practice and had banged about a bit on their drum set for a pleasant five minutes.

He also mentioned that he had been on the college volleyball and basketball teams – this was easy to believe, given his height, and later turned out to have the plus point of being true as well. When it finally hit me that he was giving me all this information in order to try and flirt with me in his own unique, subtle and slightly sardonic way, I was quite floored – here was a musical, athletic, handsome and nice older man who seemed intent on winning me over. It had seemed too good to be true.

And clearly, I now thought a tad bitterly as I struggled to unravel myself from a particularly complicated asana whose name I could no longer recall, it *had* indeed turned out to be too good to be true.

The lad was already talking marriage. Talk about killing a perfectly good romance.

Typical.

2

The First Date

Vijay was due back in Bangalore later the same day, at 8 p.m. It was about 7 p.m. when it struck me that it would be nice to surprise him by going to the airport to pick him up. I realized with a little start of guilt that every single time in the last three months that I'd had to travel on work, he had picked me up or dropped me off at the airport – whereas it had occurred to me only now, for the first time, that I could pick him up too. Especially since my guest house, strategically chosen at a mere stone's throw from his house, was also fortuitously located a short distance away from the airport. But my sense of remorse was quickly overtaken by resentment. Just because I was an innately selfish person

– a fact that I immediately decided to blame on my faulty upbringing by my mother – it didn't mean that Vijay could go about always playing Mister Nice Guy and being all thoughtful about every little thing and making me look bad in comparison. It hit me that being cooped up in my guest house, waiting for Vijay to come back, had quite possibly addled my brain. A breath of fresh air would do me some good.

I was still in a contemplative mood as I slouched along Airport Road. Maybe Vijay acting all thoughtful and gallant was a scheme to trap me into marriage. Maybe he would start acting completely different once we got hitched. Well, I wasn't just some naive silly girl. I was a savvy woman of the world – and I wasn't going to fall into any sort of trap.

I was so wrapped up in my thoughts that I stumbled on a loose slab on the pavement and nearly fell into an open manhole. After loudly cursing the civic authorities of Bangalore, I was reminded of how I had already demonstrated my clumsy side to Vijay on various occasions and had been saved at least twice from a sudden and imminent death on a busy road by his long, steadying arm. It was kind of nice to be with a man who continued to think of me as hot stuff despite prolonged exposure to my klutziness. Besides, my own personal survival rate would possibly improve simply by virtue of having that long, steadying arm around me. These were no doubt fairly useful qualities to have in a potential husband.

Husband. Ewww.

I finally reached the entry gate to the airport and negotiated my way past the many vehicles moving at a mere crawl, until I found myself at the Arrival gate. It was crowded to the hilt, as usual. I cleared my throat, tossed my hair back and gave a few of the local men haughty looks until they meekly shuffled aside. I then proceeded to occupy a prime waiting spot near the front where I could comfortably lean on the steel bars as I waited for Vijay to make his appearance.

It was still fifteen minutes to eight. I found my mind beginning to wander again as I waited moodily, my baggy-jeaned skinny frame hunched over the bars.

Had it really been three months already? It seemed like only yesterday that we had gone out on our very first date.

When Vijay first suggested that we go out that fateful day, he did so in a deliberately casual manner. Determined to outdo him, I accepted in a manner bordering on careless indifference.

'Oh sure. Whatever. I mean, I don't care.' For good measure, I even added something along the lines of 'I go out with anyone who asks me.'

He looked at me appraisingly and I realized this hadn't sounded too good, so I deftly changed the subject. 'So where do you think we should go?'

He thought for a while and then, with a gleam in his brown eyes, he asked me, 'Would you like to see ducks?'

This was a question I had never been asked before, but I decided to just go with the flow and said in the same casual manner, 'Yes, of course.'

That afternoon, I found myself getting a little worried. I had no idea what to expect and was vaguely apprehensive that 'seeing ducks' was perhaps some sort of secret code for acts I was not yet ready for – or even worse, that he might be planning to take me to the Bangalore zoo.

That evening he picked me up from my guest house. I walked up to his car, a dark green Hyundai Accent. As I got in, he said, 'Hey, you're looking nice.' I was congratulating myself for the wise but unusual decision of wearing a skirt and applying some lipstick when he added, 'Nicer than you usually look.' My smile froze on my face, but he looked like he hadn't noticed anything amiss. I would learn later that Vijay usually said whatever popped into his head. This was always without any malice whatsoever, but still difficult for a slightly oversensitive person, like me, to digest. Right now, however, he appeared to be in a very happy, conversational mood, and I melted as it dawned on me that he was talking about making this a very special first date – he was planning to drive us two hours out of Bangalore to 'see ducks' at a little resort right on the Cauveri river. I settled back in my seat with a delicious feeling of anticipation, put on my seat belt and we zoomed off.

Vijay was a very skilled driver, at least as far as I could tell, with my own limited knowledge of the matter. He negotiated the city traffic with great speed and nonchalance, humming tunelessly to himself when he wasn't keeping the conversation going and swerving out of the way of oncoming buses just in the nick of time. I tried to play it cool too, restricting my display of horror to a few sharp intakes of breath whenever it looked like we were going to perish, which he did not seem to notice. Thankfully, we were soon out of the city and headed along some quieter country roads leading towards Mysore. Our destination was about mid-way between Mysore and Bangalore, a resort called Amblee.

We finally reached and I was quite delighted by my first glimpse of the quiet, scenic place. It did give the impression of being rather dilapidated and I was dimly aware that at least part of its charm at the moment was the lack of sunlight, but for now, it was quite perfect.

The promised ducks were indeed there – all four of them – in a murky little pond in the resort gardens. After paying our respects to them, we proceeded to a table set by the river that sparkled in the moonlight. There was absolutely nobody else around and we were having a pleasant, quiet conversation and getting to know each other better. Therefore, I was taken aback when after a comfortable lull, Vijay leaned over, looked me in the eye and said, 'Naam hain Vijay … Deenanath … Chauhan. Maalum?'

I had not the slightest interest in Hindi cinema till I met Vijay. Obviously, therefore, I did not know that this was a dialogue from the movie *Agneepath*, and that Vijay was trying to impress me with what he thought was an uncanny imitation of Amitabh Bachchan. I only wondered why he was suddenly whispering in a voice two octaves lower than usual. Out loud, I just politely remarked that I had always thought his last name was Sharma, not Chauhan, adding that Deenanath was a very interesting middle name, if a little old-fashioned. He was a bit demoralized by my reaction, but when he explained to me what he had been trying to do, I pretended that I had just been kidding and praised him for his unmistakable impression, possibly overdoing it a bit by saying he 'actually sounded more like Amitabh than Amitabh himself.'

After we finished our otherwise uneventful, peaceful dinner, Vijay announced that he had organized for us to do some fishing, a thought that I was quite excited by. We settled ourselves comfortably on the cool stone steps leading into the river and a friendly resort bhaiiya handed us our extremely makeshift fishing rods – which were actually two thin bamboo sticks with strings, on the ends of which dangled little hooks wrapped in bits of atta.

There we sat, the two of us, holding our charming and only slightly sad little fishing rods, and the conversation now took a more serious turn as we quietly exchanged our many divergent views on the world at large.

It was clear that despite our mutual attraction, we had many differences – he referred to himself as a 'simple man' and was easy-going, good-humoured and even-tempered. He also was a small-town boy, had been brought up as part of a conservative family in Jaipur and had a distinctly desi flavour. I, on the other hand, was a 'modern' Delhi girl who had always had a bit of a hot temper and clearly favoured Alanis over Amitabh.

He had just finished telling me about how he had always been told that he was one of the calmest and most centred people around, when he suddenly felt a tug on his fishing rod.

'BHAIIYA! BHAIIYA!' His sudden panicked screams shattered the stillness of the night. I asked him to calm down, but he babbled on rather incoherently about being a brahmin and a vegetarian and how he had never thought these sticks would ever catch a fish and that he wanted to throw it back but couldn't bring himself to touch it and anyway, he was afraid it would bite him and it looked so awful struggling there like that and so on. The friendly resort bhaiiya came back and laughingly rescued Vijay from the fish, tossing the latter back into the river whereupon it indignantly swam away. Vijay shuddered and said we should head back into town.

And that was our first date.

I was amused by this memory as I stood waiting for Vijay at the airport and couldn't stop chuckling throatily while shaking my head from side to side, causing a couple of the local men standing around me to edge away warily.

What were we *thinking*? We were so different – it would never work. And yet, here we were, carrying on regardless. What was the point? What *for*?

And then I spotted a lanky figure that stood out head and shoulders above the rest of the crowd and my heart skipped a beat. And I suddenly remembered what for.

3

I Saw the Sign

I watched Vijay walk out of the Arrivals terminal, unaware of my presence. His dark brown hair glinted in the harsh airport lights and he was simply dressed in a blue long-sleeved shirt and a pair of black pants – one of the three decent pairs that he possessed. He slid along gracefully, almost gliding and as always, he gave me the distinct impression of being a giraffe on skates, but one who had been practising with great dedication for years for some sort of championship. He looked like he was just out of college – the one and only thing that he had ever displayed any sort of vanity about.

It was only because I was observing him closely that I noted that as usual, his brown eyes were not steady but shifting about at lightning speed. He had once told me that the reason he was able to drive so well was that his eyes were never still and he was constantly looking about all over the place and was very aware of his surroundings. Of course, I started calling him shifty-eyes after that, although this rapid eye movement was barely perceptible to the naked eye of other mortals. Sure enough, those shifty eyes now cut through the colourful confusion of the airport and settled on me, even though he hadn't been expecting me. He smiled and raised his hand slightly in a cautious wave. Unlike me, he was always wary of public displays of affection. Still, for me, that little wave was sufficient to cause another tiny skip in the cardiac region and I hurried towards him.

We greeted each other with a hug, warm on my part and hurried on his, as he simultaneously tried to register exactly who in the crowd of strangers was watching us. We held hands as we walked along and I started to talk about some inane things while he steered me towards his waiting taxi. I was still chattering happily in the car, when I noticed that he hadn't said very much and was watching me in a bemused manner.

'What?' I asked warily.

'Nothing. I was just wondering if you've thought about it some more.'

I started to observe the scenery outside the window and said coldly, 'I don't know what you're talking about.'

I knew exactly what he was talking about. And he knew that I knew. And I knew that he knew that I knew. This was getting slightly complex, so I was glad when he cut into my thoughts with 'Oh come on, honey. How much do you think we'll be able to put it off anyway?'

This was too much. 'You're *rushing* me, Vijay. It's too soon for anyone to make such a big decision.'

'Arrey! But I've decided, na? I want to marry you only. So why would it take you much longer?'

'Because ... I'm just not ready.'

'And when will you be ready?'

'I don't know,' I said honestly.

Honesty is rarely rewarded in this world.

'What do you mean you don't know? And how will you know you're ready, by the way?'

I decided to adlib. 'It's one of those things, Vijay. You just *know*. I'm sure I'll just know. But please give me time.' I preempted his next question with 'At least a few more months, maybe one year.'

His face fell. I knew that this would be tough for him to digest, but I *had* to buy myself more time. A year wasn't that long. I heard him mutter, half to himself, 'I love you but I'm not really sure I want to marry you ... I don't understand this thinking ... is it supposed to be very modern or something ... aaj kal ki ladkiyan ...'

Sometimes Vijay acted like he was not only from another planet but another generation altogether. This only served to strengthen my resolve that I would wait for a long time before making any sort of commitment.

He stopped talking about it, clearly having decided not to pursue the matter any further. Instead, he rolled down his window and produced a cigarette. I watched incredulously as he lit up in front of me, knowing fully well that I absolutely abhorred his smoking. I decided to give him the royal ignore, which would probably have worked well if he hadn't started giving it to me first, and turned away from him to look out the window. The taxi was crawling along in the traffic – it would have been quicker to walk.

As we sat there in a moody, smoky silence, I thought bitterly that maybe it would even take *two* years before I knew I was ready.

Three months had clearly not been enough, in any case. My mind began to wander over the various small incidents that had taken place over the past few months.

Unlike Vijay's pretence of being some sort of champion solo drummer in college in a lame bid to impress me, I had always let him see the real me. Take it or leave it types.

The only time I had stretched the truth *slightly* was one morning when he said that he had to go out for a haircut. Since we were at that happy lover's stage where every minute apart is seen as a minute wasted, I told him that I was great at cutting people's hair.

'Really?' he asked and I replied that I had been quite the lady in demand when it came to haircuts in my earlier days.

What I omitted to mention to him was that I had been in demand *one* day when I was ten years old – and that it was only my mother who was demanding to know where I was hiding, after a rather unfortunate haircut that I had given my younger sister. The result had come out rather uneven, although I stoutly maintained that I had intended it that way and that I quite liked it. As I had crouched in the cupboard of my room, listening to my little sister's inconsolable wailing and my mother shouting for me, I had understood even at that early age, that I was destined to be something of a misunderstood genius.

After hearing about my supposed expertise with the scissors, Vijay eagerly asked me to give him a cool haircut. I said, with an appealing combination of generosity and modesty, 'Sure, why not?'

He sat on a tall stool in the bathroom and I assumed a professional stance behind him. He was gazing into the mirror so I didn't dare to touch the front much, but I snipped away happily at the back, pausing to admire the effect now and then. I gave him an attractive series of about five steps on the back of his head. He couldn't see it, but when he reached back to touch it, he said it 'felt nice' and that he had never had this kind of haircut before.

He went happily to office the next day, clearly expecting some admiration for his new haircut, but the general reaction was summed up for him by an unnecessarily outspoken colleague who informed him that it looked as if 'kisi billi ne noch-noch ke baal nikaale hain.' Vijay was not very amused by this and over the next few days in office, could not keep from self-consciously covering the back of his head with his hand. To my chagrin, he never let me come near his hair again, even when I offered to 'fix it by snipping a bit off the back and evening out the layers.'

Our different temperaments also resulted in many fights. Given his tendency to make silly wisecracks and say whatever he felt like all the time, I often flared up about something that he did or said.

At the time, Vijay's elder brother Ajay and his wife Garima were living with Vijay and I got along well with them. They had been witnesses to quite a few of our fights, which usually ended in my flouncing out of the house. I discovered that they usually took my side, especially Ajay, who would always explain to Vijay, 'Tu bada hain. Tujhe samajhna chahiye.' Quite sweet of him, I thought, and my heart would warm to Ajay when Vijay reported this to me.

One late night, Garima found Vijay sitting on the balcony of the flat, staring forlornly at the children's playground below. When she asked what he was doing, he pointed to a lone figure sitting on one of the children's swings and said, 'Yashodhara. She's angry with me again.'

Garima breathed, 'Oh how sweeeeet.' Vijay stared at her in incredulous annoyance. It was anything but sweet, according to him.

It had all started with a casual remark he made about one of my favourite kurtas – an ethnic looking black-and-yellow long-sleeved, beaded number that I often wore with my jeans. I had always been under the impression that I looked really cool in it, but Vijay had lovingly asked me, with no small degree of interest, while toying with the beads, 'Tell me, na – why do you always wear this Hare-Rama-Hare-Krishna kind of stuff?'

It was all downhill from there and ended with my walking out of the house in a huff.

Not having any place to go so late at night, I headed to the playground, thinking that I would console myself with a little swing. A few minutes passed and I was sniffing and feeling very sorry for myself when Vijay suddenly materialized out of the black night, holding two Orange Bar ice lollies, one of which he held out to me. I took it without a word and he sat on the swing next to me with the other ice lolly, saying, 'Garima said we fight like kids, so we should make up like kids too.' We ate our ice lollies on the swings in philosophical silence and went back upstairs after a while.

He rarely lost his composure. Only once, when I had started getting upset about some small thing, he had announced, 'I'm telling you, I don't know how to deal with such tamper tentrums.' It was then that I discovered his tendency to lose his already tenuous command over the English language in moments of high emotion. He kept repeating the phrase 'tamper tentrums', obviously not spotting any flaw in it, until I finally melted and broke down in a fit of laughter. He thought I had lost it until I breathlessly explained to him why I was laughing. Thereafter, we often used the words 'tamper tentrum' to try and lighten the most unpleasant moments of conflict. Sometimes it worked.

As our taxi pulled to a stop, I briefly debated with myself whether to try and use this phrase to lighten the mood, but decided against it. The blatant smoking in my face was really the limit. Maybe, I thought as I moodily slammed the cab door behind me and stomped towards his flat, it would take me *three* years to decide. Who knew?

We had a quiet dinner at his place with Ajay and Garima. We routed most of our conversation through that hapless couple, addressing each other only a few times with exaggerated and dangerous politeness. Once in our room, we simply turned our backs on each other. I was only pretending to be asleep – I really wanted to talk to him and make up but just as I finally turned around to do so, he let out a gentle snore. I tried to shake him awake and whispered with increasing loudness, 'Vijay. VIJAY!' but he was out like a light. Irritated, I turned my back on him again and grumbling to myself, tried to go to sleep. It took me a long time.

I woke up late the next morning, the bright sunlight hurting my eyes. I licked my dry lips and realized that I was feeling very sick. It was probably my lunch of leftover Maggi and chips the previous day that had done me in, because my stomach was hurting terribly and I felt nauseous and weak.

This was the first occasion in the past few months that I had fallen sick and so I had not yet discovered Vijay's weakness for tending to the sick. He immediately forgot all about our differences of the previous day and started to fuss over me in a way that even my mother had never done.

He asked me whether I wanted to eat something and I

replied in the negative – I was feeling too sick and didn't think I would be able to keep anything down.

'But how will you regain your strength if you don't eat?' he chided.

It was kind of cute at first, but then it started to get a bit out of hand. I insisted that all I wanted to do was go to sleep, but he kept fussing over me and suggesting that I eat or drink this or that and started measuring my temperature at fifteen-minute intervals. I just lay in bed with a thermometer in my mouth, while he pottered about with an enthusiasm that he had hitherto not displayed. To my horror, he even declared that he was planning to take off from work the next day – Monday – in order to nurse me back to perfect health.

He kept coming up with new and inventive ways to fuss, but it was clearly in the matter of nourishment that he felt he had found his specialization because he kept offering me all the food and drink in the house, until I finally agreed that maybe I would try something after all.

Thrilled by this first sign of success, he made me drink a huge mug of chocolate milk, reasoning that 'milk is generally good for health' and 'even if you don't eat something, it's important for you to drink and keep your fluid levels right.'

My condition showed no visible improvement. In fact, my stomach felt significantly worse after the milk, leaving me groaning and clutching my belly in agony – until he made me sit up in bed and consume a large bowl of papaya. 'I know papaya is really good for the tummy, my mother said so.' Against my better judgment, I somehow gulped down the pulpy fruit. I had never liked papaya and now started to feel even more queasy.

'You're feeling queasy?' He had the remedy for this too. He grated some ginger and asked me to chew on it, assuring me that this would make me feel better instantly. If there was anything I disliked more than papaya, it was the taste of ginger, but I was too weak to protest and began to chew on it with an air of resignation.

The wave of nausea that overcame me right after this was too strong to resist, though I gathered up enough strength to lurch towards the bathroom. I began to throw up violently into the toilet. In between bouts, I became aware that the very concerned Vijay was standing behind me and trying to help me throw up. Weakly, I tried to push him out and shut the door behind him, but he insisted on holding me up over the toilet seat, running one hand over my hair to keep it out of the way. After I finally finished throwing up, I stumbled towards the washbasin and started cleaning up. When I looked up, I caught a glimpse of both of us in the mirror. I took in my own appearance first – I looked completely washed out, my face pale, hair matted and oily and eyes red and watering. Repulsive was the word that I would have used to describe myself.

Then I caught sight of Vijay in the mirror. He was gazing at the back of my head, still stroking my hair affectionately and muttering in self-reproach, 'Oh yaar … it's my fault … I should have added some lemon juice to the ginger. That would have worked … come on, I'll make you some nimbu paani, okay?'

It was then, at that exact moment, that I *knew*.

I drew in a deep breath and my words came out with the slow exhalation. 'Okay … let's do it.'

'Okay?' he said with the same undue enthusiasm. 'Okay, you wait, I'll get it …'

'NOT the nimbu paani, you dumbo …' I hissed. 'Okay, as in … okay, let's just get *married*.'

4

Meeting the Parents

'Okay Mum … I'll talk to you later then.' I was about to hang up the phone when it occurred to me that perhaps now was as good a time as any. 'Oh, hey Mum, I'm getting married and needed to ask you – what's our caste again?'

'What??'

A tad late, I realized that there could have been a better way to break the news, so I changed it to, 'Ha ha! Surprise?'

Stony silence at the other end of the line. I knew this stony silence well. In fact, I had inherited the Great Art of this very stony silence from my own Mother Dear.

I said, 'Ma, what I meant was that I was thinking of *maybe* getting married *sometime* and wanted to talk to you about it …' I proceeded to pour my heart out about having met Vijay a few months ago and explained to her in great detail exactly what he was like.

The stony silence changed to cold *hmmms* and *achhas* over the course of the rather one-sided conversation, but by the time I had finished, I had apparently done a decent job because I got a positively lukewarm 'Achha beta, at the end of the day, it is your decision.' Her only concern was that he was so much older than me and that the family backgrounds sounded like they were rather different, considering they wanted to know about our caste.

'They don't want to know,' I hastily corrected her. 'As in, Vijay said since they don't know anything about me, they *might* want to know. But he said it's probably not relevant at all, but still, you never know. You know?'

I knew I wasn't being very convincing. The truth was I wasn't too convinced myself.

In fact, when he had tried to casually slip in the question about my caste, I had felt my hackles rise. I had told him in no uncertain terms that while I didn't have the slightest clue about my caste, if there was going to be an eighteenth-century, caste-based discussion, then he could take his high-born brahmin ass and jump off the nearest conveniently located cliff. He had tried to explain to me in an earnest, fumbling manner that while it was of zero consequence to him and *probably* of none to his parents, he just wanted to sound like he was completely prepared with all the answers. I wasn't happy about it, but after much grumbling, had finally agreed to ask my mother.

Just before we hung up, my mother agreed in a resigned manner that she would check with her own father and get back to me about our caste. I marvelled at this – clearly she and my late father hadn't cared about caste when they decided to marry and neither had their families. How different my situation was, even though it was what, like, sixty years later or something? Ah, the things we do for love, I thought, feeling quite like a Hindi movie heroine. I realized with a start that I was not only going to be somebody's wife, but somebody was perhaps even going to refer to me as 'bahu'. Holy crap! Cow, cow, holy cow, I told myself reproachfully. Had to tone down the language.

It turned out that we were from the lineage of something called Suryavanshi Rajputs – now this sounded quite cool to me. I'd always known I had a little bit of the warrior in me. I told Vijay this, adding a little bitingly that if his family had a problem with me, mine would wage war against his and beat them. He brightly said that this explained a lot and confessed that he had always privately likened me to the Jhansi ki Rani. He promised to keep my threat in mind.

The next step was for him to meet my mother and he accordingly made a trip to Delhi about a week later. He was a little nervous but I wasn't worried. I knew it would not be much of a challenge for him to win her over.

Mother Dear was a high-ranking government official – at that point, she was the Chief Comissioner of Delhi in Customs and Central Excise. To the outside world, she was a highly respected and impressive figure, bordering on the formidable. But to me and my two siblings – the elder, focused doctor-residing-in-England Abhimanyu and the younger, easygoing Gitanjali – she was just Good Ol' Mama. Generally terribly wise and sensible and capable of just about everything, but with a remarkable tendency to exhibit rather daft behaviour at times. She actually had only two primary shortcomings – which we called in the politically correct corporate world 'Areas of Improvement' – the first being an inability to admit that she was wrong and the second being an inability to tell a coherent joke or story to save her life.

It turned out that I was right in my estimation that she would highly approve of Vijay. After his visit, I had a quick conversation with my sister Gitanjali, who reported that Vijay had quite floored our mother. Almost literally, because apparently he had caught her off guard and nearly tripped her up by making a dive for her feet as soon as he entered the house. In this regard, he was old-fashioned, as was the rest of his family. It was apparently his innate niceness and almost painful shyness that won our mother over.

Gitanjali said rather gleefully, 'He kept laughing nervously and saying, "It's a pleasure, aunty … eh-eh-heh" about everything. It was funny!'

I did not approve of this fun-making of my beau, even though she was doing a good job of imitating his embarrassed mumbling and it did sound as though it had been rather amusing. I snapped, 'Stop laughing. He's going to be your brother-in-law. What did *you* think of him?'

Her response was immediate and warm. 'Oh, I thought he was very sweet!' Honesty compelled her to add, 'But a bit mad, of course.'

I narrowed my eyes and opened my mouth to refute. But I realized that I found it a fairly accurate assessment and decided to just let it go at that. Thanking my little squirt of a sister for her frank opinion, I hung up and sighed.

He had done it. However, I suspected that winning over *his* parents was not going to be so easy for me.

For one, they were from a different generation altogether – Vijay was not only much older than me, but he also happened to be the youngest of the four children, the imaginatively named quartet Rama-Shyama-Ajay-Vijay. He was the baby of the family. The one they were all the fondest of and referred to by the nickname 'Tunnu', which of course I found eminently laughable and derived great pleasure in teasing him about.

'But Ajay's pet name is Pappi,' he had pointed out vehemently.

I had doubled over in laughter all over again.

They were from Jaipur which, of course, was a very different kind of place from my hometown Delhi. Also, they were strict vegetarian brahmins and had certain ideas about the kind of daughter-in-law they wanted. It was clear to me that these certain ideas were at odds with the person that I was. Vijay assured me that they were wonderful people, but

I could see that he too had his doubts about how easily they would accept me.

I brooded on this issue for a while – the only members of his family that I had met so far were Ajay, Garima and his little nephew Praagya, nicknamed Pikki. Pikki was the son of Vijay's eldest sister – the rather ominous sounding gynae-oncological surgeon, who I always thought of as Scary Dr Rama Didi. Pikki however was a chubby-cheeked little lad, whom I had first met two months ago when he had been sent to visit Vijay for a few days in Bangalore. During his stay, we had hung out a bit and he had heard me strumming on my guitar. Being a mere eight-year-old and therefore easily impressed, he was quite taken with me. In return, I thought of him as a particularly cute and intelligent child who exhibited an obvious good taste in people.

It later transpired that when Pikki went back home, the hot topic of discussion amongst the various concerned adults in the family was the screening of prospective brides for Vijay. Some nice shiny new brahmin girl from Jaipur was apparently one of the frontrunners and young Pikki could not stop himself from piping up with a scornful challenge, 'But can she play the guitar?' This statement had the effect of mystifying his parents completely – and later, when we got to know about it, of amusing Vijay and doubling my admiration for young Pikki.

I now found myself feeling anxious as Vijay was travelling from Delhi to Jaipur to have the Talk with his parents. Just a couple of years before, Ajay and Garima had been married through the conventional arranged route and Vijay's parents were clearly expecting him to go the same way. Now that it was clear that we wanted to get hitched, he felt they needed to be primed accordingly, so that they would be happy about our decision.

I didn't realize at the time that Vijay had chosen to arm himself with a couple of things he had sneakily taken from my files as a first step towards winning over his parents. One was an unusual picture of me at my recent convocation from management school, where I was dressed in a sari – one of the few occasions I had consented to wear what I considered a particularly painful and wretched garment. I was standing straight and tall, smiling brightly right at the camera, my shoulder-length dark brown hair shampooed and blow-dried, looking slim and elegant in the light blue sari that my visiting mother had helped me don. In other words, I looked nothing like my usual skinny, grungy and hunched-up self.

The other item that he took to show his father was the resumé that I had prepared for placement season at B-School. It had been suitably crafted to impress any prospective employer with my various wonderful professional qualities. Little did I know that he would cunningly swipe it to impress his father, a retired professor of physics, who Vijay knew would be pleased to see my impeccable academic qualifications from the best institutes in the country. Later, when I found out about this, I shook my head in disbelief – the whole set-up seemed completely alien to me, almost surreal.

During his all-important visit to Jaipur to break the news about me, Vijay did all the priming and question-fielding and truth-stretching required, smoothly assuring his parents and elder sisters that I would fit very well into the family and they would see that for themselves when they met me.

I had pounced on him for all the details once he returned from this trip and had been listening with great interest to his account of his conversation with them when he reached this point. My voice came out in an unnaturally high-pitched squeak. '*Meet* them? Already?'

Two weeks later, I was a nervous wreck as we flew out from Bangalore to Jaipur for this fateful meeting. As luck would have it, the food on our Indian Airlines flight was so singularly stale that the non-vegetarian meal that I consumed to fortify myself caused me to develop an immediate and severe case of food poisoning. This was the second instance in the last few weeks that my stomach had failed me, the bitter irony of it being that prior to meeting Vijay, this had never happened to me. Most of the next few hours passed in a blur, but I was aware of a few things – high fever and giddiness; the concerned look on Vijay's face; the memory of how he had acted when I had fallen ill earlier and consequently a vague sort of worry at the back of my mind that the ghost of Florence Nightingale might re-enter his body and he would start to feed me his special, vomit-inducing combination of Horlicks, papaya and grated ginger.

He somehow managed to get me into a taxi when we landed at Jaipur and on the way to his parents' house, I kept deliriously repeating in a conversational tone, 'Honey, you know what? Your family is going to absolutely hate me!' For some reason, this thought struck me as pretty funny and I added, 'Wheee! Ha ha!'

'No, no, of course they won't,' Vijay assured me a few times, his voice uncertain.

As our taxi wove its way towards his home, he said, 'Er, you remember what we discussed about speaking only in Hindi to Mummyji, right?'

'Of course,' I retorted dizzily. 'I can do Hindi. Hindi is my mother's tongue.' Then a feeling of sudden panic hit me and I demanded, 'Quick! How do you say namaste in Hindi?'

Vijay said something in response, but at this point, I fell asleep against his shoulder.

I woke up just as we reached their house, a nice little one-storeyed grey structure in an old colony of Jaipur, situated opposite a well-maintained park. I had, as a concession to the big occasion, worn a salwar-kameez. I was completely overwhelmed. There were many people milling around; I had never done this sort of thing before; I had no idea what to expect and felt like my every move was being watched and judged. On top of this, the fever seemed to be peaking and I was dimly aware of the fact that I wasn't thinking or speaking very clearly.

It was a crowded house because Vijay's sisters and Ajay, along with their respective spouses, had also landed up to grace the occasion. Vijay had told me that they always greeted each other with the younger people touching the feet of the older lot. I was the youngest person around for miles. This meant that, as soon as I walked in, there were many pairs of feet for me to bend over and touch respectfully. This was also something I had never done before and had only seen in movies, but I just followed Vijay's lead and once I got into the flow, it felt nice and theatrical. 'Pau laagu Maaji!' I thought, as I touched my prospective mother-in-law's feet. 'Pau laagu Bauji,' I murmured as I touched Papaji's feet. In a fit of enthusiasm, I found myself bending over to grab the feet of everybody in sight, being stopped by Vijay just in the nick of time from also embracing those of Murugan, the old family servant, who stood looking on curiously from somewhere at the periphery of all the mayhem.

After this, I smiled beatifically at everybody throughout the remainder of the visit and answered all the questions directed at me. I remembered and followed Vijay's advice that one of the keys to Mummyji's heart would be to converse with her in Hindi. She was a small lady who seated herself next to me on the sofa, observing me keenly with unexpectedly striking grey eyes. All her children were above average height, clearly having taken after Papaji in this regard. Just to make some conversation, I was about to remark on how amazing it was that four such tall, strapping adults could have been produced by such a tiny being as her, but thought the better of it. Or more accurately, by the time I finished doing an acceptable translation of the thought in my head into Hindi without sounding hopelessly vulgar, I had forgotten all about it.

Now, Mummyji was saying something to me which I had missed. I concentrated hard and realized she had just asked me whether my elder brother was already married. I was dazed, but I knew the answer to this one. Giving her what I hoped was a winning smile, I informed her in no uncertain terms, 'Yes. Aur Bhabhiji bhi bahut acchi hain – bilkul meri tarah!' There was a moment of silence and then the whole room burst into laughter, while I looked around and blinked at everybody in a confused but good-natured way.

Vijay had informed them that I was very ill and therefore not my usual dazzling self. Either way, despite the fever – or perhaps because of it – his family accepted our decision to marry. A month later, my mother came over with me and Vijay to Jaipur for a visit to meet them and a date towards the end of February was fixed.

My mother had been a tad indignant when, towards the end of her visit, Papaji voiced his request that there be no alcohol and non-vegetarian food at our wedding. 'What do they think, we are some kind of barbarians or something? Of course there will be no alcohol and non-veg food at the wedding,' she said when we were back in Delhi. I couldn't quite muster up the courage to point out that this conversation was happening over the carcass of a delicious but unfortunate chicken and a glass of wine. I was always up for a good debate, but not with my mother, who was a worse loser of arguments than even I was.

In any case, I was just happy and relieved that both sides had been successfully convinced to approve of our impending marriage. Also, one of my newfound principles in life: you don't argue with your mother, especially when she is generously springing the cash for your wedding. At least, not until after the wedding.

5

Marrying a Sharma

The wedding was a fairly low-key affair at the Radisson hotel in Delhi. It would perhaps have been a little higher-key if all of my friends had shown up, but unfortunately, a lot of them were scattered across the country and worldwide. Apparently the notice that I gave them – ranging from about two weeks to five days before the wedding, depending on who I remembered when – was not good enough for many of them to make the trip. Instead, they sent their love and best wishes for the both of us with a few choice abuses just for me. The argument I used in my defense, that I had never been married before and it was all very new to me, did not cut much ice with them.

As always, blood proved to be thicker than friends and most of my family, also scattered all over the world, *did* make it to the ceremonies – also due to the fact that my mother had handled their invitations and had apparently informed them about a month in advance. So my favourite cousin Mini had flown in from Australia and was flashing her dimpled smile all over the place; my brother Abhimanyu and his wife Vandna had landed up, flying in all the way from England.

My make-up was done by a distant relative whom we called Mrignaina mausi, who was a make-up artist by profession. She had been overly enthusiastic, caking on layers and layers of stuff on my face and sticking about sixty-seven pins into some sort of fake bun on my head. I was itching to get away from her expert hands and was fervently wishing that this distant relative would make herself distant again, but just as I was on the verge of tearing out of the room screaming, she said, 'There! All done!'

I looked at myself and I had to admit that she had done a really good job. I looked quite stunning. I wouldn't go out to the market like this, but for my wedding it seemed just about right. My pale pink and silver sari, which I had insisted on as opposed to the usual red or maroon varieties, shimmered delicately around my person. The fake hairbun didn't look half bad either. My mother took one look at me and a little tear started to form in the corner of her eye, but she stopped herself from making any sort of impulsive display by somehow finding a stray hair and tucking it behind my ear in a business-like manner. I just grinned at her cheekily, for once refraining from protesting at this gesture. It was okay. I understood how she felt.

It was finally time to make my appearance in the wedding hall. I waited outside the door, concentrating on not tripping on my sari. Vandna was accompanying me, and just as the door opened, she whispered, 'There is no need to smile so much.' This remark confused me for a moment, considering that this was supposed to be the happiest day of my life and all that, but I quickly deciphered that it meant she thought I should be a bit more of the coy, blushing bride. I obeyed her and managed a fairly sombre expression, although it was quite an effort when I caught sight of Vijay.

He had been refusing to behave like the typical groom and had been wandering all around the large hall, greeting old friends and long-lost family members – much to the consternation of Rama didi, who had a very strong sense of propriety and was unsuccessfully pursuing him through the crowd in order to inform him that he should really be sitting still on one of the two chairs on the platform. When the door opened to reveal me and I started walking in slowly, everybody turned to look at me with gratifying oohs and aahs.

Vijay, who at that point had been merrily chatting with some old friends from IIT, also joined the crowd as they all turned to look at the coy, blushing and no doubt radiant bride. He stood there, transfixed, along with everybody else, watching me in this strange new avatar. As I walked, I kept my eyes mostly lowered but I spotted him through the heavily mascaraed lashes and had to bite my lower lip to keep from laughing at the expression of pure admiration on his face.

He continued to stand there with a silly grin until Rama didi finally caught up to him and urged him to take his place on the platform. He reached it and quickly sat down just a few seconds before I did, but the serene smile on his face as I reached him gave the impression that he had been fixed in his seat, waiting patiently for me for the last hour or so.

It was as he stood up to welcome me that I got my first close look at him for the evening. Instantly, I realized that I could have done a better job of helping him with his wedding suit – the silver-white sherwani that he had got tailored for himself was too broad at the shoulders and combined with his height, his skinny legs and the bright red turban on his head gave him the uncanny appearance of a larger-than-life tube of Colgate toothpaste. I could almost see the words inscribed near the base: 'For Best Results, Squeeze from Bottom Up'. I was unable to retain the sombre expression that Vandna had imposed upon me and started to laugh. I had to pretend to have a coughing fit to disguise my giggles. He sat next to me, giving me the odd quizzical glance now and then, but otherwise resplendent and elegant, as much as human toothpaste tubes could be.

After this, a lot of people, most of whom we didn't know, came up to us to wish us well, hand us gifts and envelopes stuffed with cash and have photographs taken with us. The photographer was possibly the most annoying photographer in the world, creating blinding flashes when we least expected them and constantly telling me, 'Up your chin, up your chin, madam.' After a while, every time he said this, I started to mutter under my breath, 'Up yours, sir!'

He then started repeatedly saying between flashes, 'Madam, can you more down? Sir, can you more up?' I was about to tell him off, but then I saw that he had a point. While sitting, for some reason, I looked taller than Vijay.

This realization came as an immense shock to me, as his six feet two inches usually dwarfed my five feet six and a half inches. I asked him to stop slouching and sit up, but even when he straightened his back completely, I was still taller than him. Why had I never noticed this before?

I hissed at him, 'Oh my *god*. You have a freakishly short upper body!'

A few people who were standing near the podium turned around to look at us. I immediately looked down coyly and started examining the mehendi on my hands. An annoyed Vijay whispered back to me, 'Or maybe, *you* have freakishly short legs. How about that?'

I mumbled that I had a longish upper body and average length legs. Still, this wouldn't do, our wedding photos were mostly of us sitting next to each other and I was now sure that we looked silly like this. So I whispered a suggestion to Vijay about lifting up his red pagdi slightly. For the rest of the photographs, I slouched as much as I could while Vijay straightened up with his pagdi perched higher on his head. These simple steps resulted in giving the camera the correct impression that he was taller than me. The only glitch was that he now looked like a Colgate toothpaste tube whose cap had been screwed on too loosely, but I figured this was a small price to pay and wisely refrained from pointing it out to him.

The greet-and-photo session went on and on. We got so used to saying 'Thank you' with fake smiles plastered on our faces that, when one gentleman said, 'I'm Dr Gulati, an old friend of your mother-in-law,' Vijay gave him his best fake smile, shook his hand firmly and replied, 'Thank you, uncle.'

Eventually, it was time for the pheras – the ceremony where we walked around the fire and the punditji droned on and on about our vows. It was late, almost 2 a.m., and Punditji was explaining the meaning of each of the vows to us. I tried very hard to listen to him, but I was actually stifling yawns the whole time. I had been sitting cross-legged for a long time on the floor and it was very uncomfortable. At one point, to my horror, I thought I felt my sari giving me a wedgie, but it thankfully turned out be a false alarm. I only woke from my stupor when Punditji said that, as part of the ceremony, Vijay and I should feed each other laddoos, which sounded to me like the most sensible thing he'd said all night. He asked Vijay to go first. I turned towards him and lifted my face up with a coy smile. Vijay broke off a piece of laddoo just the right size and I opened my mouth expectantly. Ignoring me completely, he proceeded to swiftly pop the laddoo into his own mouth, much to the merriment of the many observers and to the chagrin of Punditji, as apparently this marred the ritual that denotes the sharing of every aspect of our lives. I accepted Vijay's next offering rather haughtily. Clearly, he was not taking this sacred ritual seriously enough and was paying even less attention to Punditji's instructions than I was. In the background, I was aware of my cousin Mini and sister Gitanjali holding on to each other in a fit of helpless laughter, but I pretended I didn't find it the least bit funny.

It was finally over and we were married. The vidai was something of a sham because we were spending the night at the Radisson. So we were being seen off, only to circle around for a block or two before coming back. I bid everybody farewell very cheerfully, deliberately keeping my distance from Vandna, who would no doubt tell me to attempt to cry or something. It was only much later, while watching our wedding video, that I discovered that my obvious merriment looked very out of place, but only because the enthusiastic video-maker had bunged in at this point a particularly weepy song about the sadness of a young bride leaving her family to join an unfamiliar one. The music formed a strange contrast to the candid shots of me with a wide grin on my face, blowing kisses and waving happily to all and sundry.

When we finally got back to our hotel room, Vijay answered the ringing phone. It was the hotel management asking if everything was to our satisfaction. Vijay answered that indeed it was. The man said, 'Thank you, Mister Lal,' and hung up.

Vijay did not see the humour in this, although I explained that it was probably a simple misunderstanding since my mother had done the room booking. My little joke of 'What, you don't intend to change your surname to mine now?' didn't go down too well either.

Before we put the lights out, my mother called to check if everything was okay with us. I lay back, exhausted after the day we'd had, lazily listening to their exchange.

Vijay said warmly, 'Thank you, aunty – for everything.'

I heard my mother's voice chiming from the receiver, chiding him, 'Beta, I'm your mother now. So call me mama from now on, okay? No more of this aunty-shanty.'

Vijay laughed self-deprecatingly, 'Sure, I'll remember.'

Mother continued, 'So we'll talk tomorrow. Goodnight, beta.'

'Goodnight, aunty.' And with that, my brand-new husband hung up the phone.

6

The Honeymoon

A couple of days after the wedding, we took off on our honeymoon. Vijay and I devised our very own personal welcome slogan and sang out in childish excitement as our flight landed, 'Welcome to Goooaaaa!'

The first couple of days unfolded beautifully. We stayed in a cottage-home at a Taj property and went walking along the spotless beaches. The resort's swimming pool had an inbuilt bar, so we splashed around after sipping Bloody Marys and beer. We rented a bike and rode around exploring the place, Vijay expertly manoeuvering the vehicle along side roads with me hanging on for dear life, happier than I had ever been before, with my arms wrapped tight around his skinny – and freakishly short – upper body. We tried the feni and resolved never to try it again and went to all the happening joints and beaches and some of the shady ones too. At the flea market, we bought packets and packets of cheap items, including large straw hats and bright shirts that screamed 'I'm a tourist' and which we knew we would never wear after his trip.

It was on the third day that we decided to take the bike all the way to Dudhsagar waterfalls, at the other end of Goa. We rode for five hours, refuelling several times on the way. The last seven kilometres were on a poorly maintained dirt track through a forest. My teeth rattled as I held on to Vijay's flimsy touristy shirt, trying to keep from being thrown off the bike. We finally made it, sweaty and tired – but triumphant. We had only a small climb over some rocks to get to the waterfalls when Vijay suddenly spotted a small monkey innocently scratching itself nearby. Screeching like a teenage girl, he announced rather incoherently that we had to go back *right now*. Upon my questioning him, I discovered that he had some sort of phobia of wild monkeys. We were so close that we could hear the waterfalls, but he refused to move closer to them and stood frozen on the spot, staring fearfully at the small lone monkey. This was too much for me. I dragged him bodily past the monkey towards the waterfalls, barking in his ear, 'We came here to see the waterfalls and we're going to see the waterfalls even if we get our eyes scratched out. Now ENJOY yourself!'

The waterfalls were pretty, but the presence of some drunk locals marred the romantic scenery, as did Vijay's nervous shifty-eyed glancing about for the tiny monkey. After about ten minutes, we set off on the five-hour journey back to the hotel. Overall, this outing was a definite adventure. Not at all worth it, of course.

The next day was shaping up to be much more promising – we were going to try our hand at adventure sports. After a brief discussion, we decided we would go jet-skiing and parasailing.

The jet-skiing was first – we rented two jet-skis and we were each to be accompanied by expert jet-skiers who would do the actual steering. We took off, Vijay's jet-ski one split second before mine, and my heart jumped into my throat at how fast we were going. We were riding the waves as if the ocean was one bumpy, blue road. After a while, Vijay even tried his hand at driving his jet-ski. I didn't dare try it myself because it looked difficult. Also, I didn't want to trouble my instructor too much, because just a few minutes into the ride, I had snapped my head back suddenly to ask him something and had ended up ramming his jaw very hard. After that, he might have been a bit annoyed with me, because he had stopped speaking to me – or perhaps he just couldn't talk any more.

I was extremely excited about the next item on the agenda: parasailing. I was sure it was going to be even more thrilling and hurried a protesting Vijay through lunch, leaving my own plate nearly untouched.

There was only one other couple ahead of us. The man

seemed on the obnoxious side. The instructor kept repeating, 'Just remember to pull down to the *right* when you see me wave the red flag – pull *right*, okay? This motion will bring you down here on this spot and you'll be fine.'

'Wow – it's really that simple? Come on, come on then, let's go,' said Mr Obnoxious impatiently.

He and his wife, whom I felt rather sorry for, were going ahead of us. Vijay and I were strapped onto the sail and just before our boat was to take off with us in tow, we were asked to remove our shoes. I threw off my slippers carelessly and then realized the sand was burning hot. In a hurry, I started trying to run, dragging the sail with me, while Vijay was forced to lope along behind me, saying, 'Wait, wait.' I hopped on one foot and then the other and thankfully the boat started up and zoomed off and we found ourselves taking off into the air.

We went sailing higher and higher and when I looked down, the sight of the sea, the beach and the trees far below us was breathtaking and frightening. I wanted to squeeze Vijay's hand and savour the moment, but since we were both hanging on for dear life, I decided I would save the hand-squeezing for later. He was trying to whisper something possibly very romantic into my ear, but I couldn't hear anything over the rushing wind. He then tried shouting but I still couldn't hear him, so he finally just gave up and we sailed together through the bright blue sky. I felt like we were getting closer and closer to the hot sun. It was perfect.

Like all good things, it was over too soon and our boat began to veer towards the beach. I spotted the instructor waving his red flag frantically and pointed at him, but Vijay was apparently already on top of it. He pulled down towards the right with all his might and we were soon headed to a safe landing on the beach.

We landed and I realized that, while it had been great fun, I was feeling especially thrilled to be back on solid ground. As we were being helped out of our sail, we became aware of some commotion nearby. It seems that when he saw the instructor waving, Mr Obnoxious had pulled down with all his considerable weight, except he did it to the *left* and had thus made a perfect landing in the ocean. We looked over and spotted him and his poor wife being fished out of the water, both sputtering at the indignity and unfairness of it all.

I would have enjoyed it a lot more if the hot sand had not once again been burning holes into my soles and I went hopping over to retrieve my slippers as quickly as I could.

The honeymoon was over. The flight back to Bangalore was delayed and we landed in the city late at night. Although physically exhausted, we chattered endlessly about how we would do up our place together, what we needed to buy and so on. It was only when we reached home and were paying off the taxi driver that I realized something was missing.

'Honey, where's our luggage?'

'Huh?'

I was aghast at what we had done. The two of us were so accustomed to day trips as part of our marketing jobs that we had each brought back only our little carry-on bags slung over our shoulders and had forgotten to collect the rest of our luggage from baggage claim. A perfectly understandable error, except that what we had forgotten were four large suitcases laden with wedding gifts.

We got the taxi driver to take us back and eventually found our suitcases sitting near the conveyer belt, being examined by two airport officials who eyed us suspiciously as we explained how we had just happened to leave so many large pieces of luggage behind. They were clearly on the fence, wavering between whether to believe us or to call for back-up in case we were crazies who posed some sort of security threat – until Vijay sidled up to them and whispered coyly, 'Please excuse. Just married.'

We were granted permission to retrieve our luggage and we headed home.

7

Settling Down

'Vijay! My wedding jewellery ... it's gone!'

It was the third day after our return to Bangalore and we were still unpacking and putting things away when I decided to take a look at the bag of jewellery that we had bunged into our bedroom cupboard the night we arrived. To my shock and dismay, I found several pieces of jewellery missing.

I had never really owned anything but junk jewellery before and had received, as wedding gifts, several expensive and beautiful pieces gifted by various generous people, although I was utterly confused about who had given what. Naturally, I was now disheartened and lamented the heavy loss, not even daring to calculate how much of a loss it actually was.

Vijay comforted me to the best of his ability. He also played the part of the Angry Young Husband to a T, vowing to put locks upon our cupboards and casting a suspicious eye on the cooking maid, the cleaning maid and even the monkeys that occasionally hung around on the trees outside our balcony. I said in a martyred fashion that it didn't matter and that we couldn't just go about accusing people, or for that matter, simians, without proof; and that perhaps, in retrospect, a plastic bag in an unlocked cupboard was not the best place to house wedding jewellery and therefore it was at least partly our own fault. It was something that we just had to bear with fortitude, even if it meant that the symbols of the happiest day of my life were now gone forever. I ended my speech with a melodramatic sigh and I could see Vijay was impressed. We agreed not to tell our family, especially my mother, who had worked so hard to make the wedding a success. Let her, I said, bask in the afterglow of my successful, without-a-single-notable-mishap wedding for a few days – we would bear this heavy burden ourselves.

We kept quiet about it in conversations with the family. However, now that we had rejoined work, I discovered that for reasons best known to himself, Vijay seemed to have spread the story far and wide amongst our colleagues. So whenever someone congratulated me on the wedding, they also added in hushed tones a few words of consolation about the loss of *all* my wedding jewellery. I was constantly trying to forget about it but every time someone brought it up, I had no choice but to put on a sad face that mirrored their expressions and agree with them while they tutted about what the world was coming to when a young bride lost *all* her wedding jewellery so soon after the wedding.

After a few days of this drama, I finally decided to break the news to my mother on the phone, hurriedly adding that it was only very expensive jewellery after all and she should therefore not take it to heart.

'Oh, I won't take it to heart,' she promised, but being the perceptive sort, I detected a note of sarcasm in her voice.

She went on to sternly inform me that the jewellery pieces were missing simply because they had been left behind by me in her house in Delhi and she had been waiting for me to bring it up when I finally noticed.

I was both relieved and stung by this revelation. I said that my leaving the jewellery behind was a little inadvertent slip. She said it was carelessness of the highest order and asked me if I even knew which of the pieces were missing.

Hurt to the quick by this, I retorted that while I didn't have the slightest clue about the actual pieces missing, I was well aware that the sheer volume had been reduced by about sixty per cent.

She said tartly that jewellery was not usually measured by 'sheer volume' and suggested that perhaps it would be a good idea for her to put it all in a locker in Delhi. I saw the sense in this and agreed.

'So, what do you think we should buy first for the flat?'

It was our first Sunday back and we were contemplating finally doing up the place a bit. We were staying at the same flat that Vijay had been living in earlier, in a posh complex on Airport Road. Ajay and Garima had moved to the US a few months earlier. I really missed having them around at home and also wondered who would talk sense into Vijay about every fight we had being his fault.

The flat was a nice and airy one, with two large bedrooms, a fair-sized kitchen and a lovely sunny balcony. I turned in a slow circle, taking in the bare drawing room. I thought about it and suggested, 'Well, most people have curtains. Maybe we should start with those.'

Despite months of Garima's presence and civilizing influence, Vijay hadn't bothered to get a single curtain for the apartment so far. This contributed to the feeling of openness and let in plenty of air and sun, but I soon convinced him that a few curtains would be a good idea. I cleverly included the fact that with curtains in place, he wouldn't have to

look at the monkeys that swung on the trees right outside
the balcony and occasionally peeped into the house. He
shuddered and agreed.

Vijay went in for a bath and while he was thus occupied,
I thought it would be a good idea to surprise him with his
favourite breakfast of alu-parathas. How wifely of me. I felt a
strange sort of satisfaction and went into the kitchen to look
around for the ingredients.

During a short visit to Jaipur just before the wedding,
I had carefully observed how his mother made the alu-
parathas for him, stuffing them lovingly with alu-masala
consisting of surprising amounts of lal-mirchi and dhania. I
had memorized the methodology pretty well – but now I just
couldn't find what I needed.

When Vijay came out of his bath, he found me standing
in the middle of the kitchen, looking desolate. 'What
happened? You need something?'

'Honey,' I was petulant because my surprise was being
spoilt, 'I thought I'd make you some nice alu-parathas. But
you don't have any atta in the house!'

'Of course there is atta – did you look in this cupboard
over here?' He opened the cupboard I was standing in front
of and pulled out a large blue packet. 'See? Right here, a new
packet.'

'This?' I was genuinely surprised 'What are you talking
about? This is not the type of atta I mean. Where is the sticky
stuff we make rotis with?'

There was a moment of silence. Vijay put his arm around
me gently. 'I know you haven't cooked before. But please tell
me you know that atta doesn't come readymade in the form
you use for rotis?'

I felt my face getting hot. Of course I knew that –

somewhat vaguely. It was just that I wasn't used to this whole kitchen gig and had merely blanked out for a minute there.

Still, it wouldn't do to have my husband think of me as a total idiot. So I forced myself to laugh. 'Ha ha! Don't be silly. Who wouldn't know *that*?'

This incident would make me the butt of many jokes later, but its more immediate effect over the next few days was that Vijay took it upon himself to try and teach me how to cook. I wasn't an enthusiastic student, but soon I was able to make tea, alu-parathas and artistically misshapen rotis, of which – just like snowflakes – no two were ever alike.

Dal continued to be a challenge, however. It would always end up spilling out of the pressure cooker, possibly because I always ended up putting in the wrong amount of water.

'I told you – you're supposed to put in three times as much water as the dal,' Vijay said, leaning against the kitchen doorway one morning, as I stood with a frown of concentration in front of the open pressure cooker. 'How much dal have you just put in?'

'Two fistfuls.'

He looked at me for a moment and then said, 'Okay, fine – so just put in six fistfuls of water now.' As he walked away, I could hear him muttering, 'Beyond a point, I can't help …'

8

Going Shopping

Over the next few weeks, life became extremely busy. At work, I had just been assigned to manage one of the 'most important Premium Dust Tea brands in South India', which was a hugely profitable cash cow for the company but which, being a North Indian from 'Dahli', I had never actually heard of until I was informed that I was now the brand manager for it. Vijay had rejoined in his earlier capacity as marketing manager in the foods category and was back to sardonically interviewing embarrassed housewives in order to dream up ways to get them to stuff their kids with items like jam and squash – items which he himself never touched.

We used every spare moment on the weekends to do the shopping in order to set up our home. We had first gone out to buy curtains. As expected, our tastes were fairly different, but we figured it was okay because curtains had to be purchased for all the rooms in the house. We went around happily indulging our individual tastes – I bought light, flowing pinks and oranges and he went for heavier, more staid greys and blues. It was only later, when we actually got around to putting them up, that we realized that the various sizes we had bought for different windows now resulted in each room in our house having to be adorned in a combination of our clashing tastes, resulting in an interesting overall effect. The drawing room was now done up in mera waala light pink and his grey-and-blue. I decided I quite liked it.

'We should buy blue sofas, I think,' I announced after stepping back and running a critical eye over the room.

To my surpirse, Vijay agreed. 'Haan, you're right. That will bring it all together very nicely. Bright blue, right?'

The thought occurred to me that possibly, most people bought sofa sets and other furniture first and then decided on matching curtains – but I brushed it aside as being such a *common* approach. 'Bright blue,' I affirmed.

When I had talked to Vijay earlier about our need for sofas, stating my personal belief in having some sort of seating arrangement apart from mattresses and beanbags, he had readily agreed. However, one of the criteria he was adamant about was that it should not 'sweat' – by which he meant that since he planned to sleep on it while I was travelling, it should be of a material that would not make him hot and sweaty during the night. So we agreed that we were on the lookout for bright-blue, non-sweating sofas.

These turned out to be harder to come by than you might expect.

Over the next few days, I suggested that we relax the colour criteria since sofas appeared to be available in most hues other than blue. But apparently Vijay had boundless energy when it came to 'studying the options' while shopping, so we continued to systematically explore what felt like every furniture shop in Bangalore.

To my increasing chagrin, I was discovering the incompatibility in our shopping styles, which applied to every item that we considered buying. While I usually wanted to grab the first reasonable facsimile of whatever we had in mind and get out of the shop as fast as I could, Vijay wanted to research *everything*. He had an obsession with having 'options' and for every single item on our list, he would not rest until he had examined and evaluated at least four alternatives. This habit was frustrating, especially since we would invariably end up buying the very item that I had pointed out in the first place.

Vijay's thoroughness as a shopper was also proving detrimental to various unfortunate salespersons that we encountered on the way. At one store, I pointed out a nice, dark sofa made of some leather-like material. A glib salesguy swooped down on us and said, 'Ah yes, sir, ma'am. This is a great piece.'

Vijay leaned towards the sofa, leaned away from it, bent to the side to examine it and said, 'Hmmm. But does it sweat?'

The salesguy said, 'I'm sorry, sir? Sweat?'

Vijay explained, 'You know, sweat? As in, if I'm going to sleep on it all night, will it get all sweaty for me?'

The salesguy pretended to get it and started nodding wisely. 'Oh, that. Of course not, sir. It will not sweat at all.'

Vijay said 'hmmm' in a non-committal way. He then surreptitiously put his hand on the sofa and kept it there, while proceeding to ask the salesguy a series of questions about the exact nature of the material, where it was made, what the price was, the logistics, sourcing and human resource strategy of the company that made it and so on.

After a few minutes of this, just when the glib salesman thought he had sealed the deal, Vijay suddenly withdrew his hand and thrust it towards the salesman's face accusingly, saying '*You* said it would not sweat. But I kept my hand on it for five minutes and it's sweating. See?'

The salesguy recoiled at Vijay's sweaty hand. He was rendered speechless and his gaze moved between Vijay's palm and the imprint it had left behind on the expensive sofa. We left very shortly afterwards, my cheeks red.

Thankfully, the sofa ordeal eventually ended when we lucked out with a new shipment at Gautier – a sofa set that was not only bright blue, but as soft as you might expect the clouds to be. Once you sank onto the sofa, it was difficult to escape and Vijay and I would later spend many pleasant Sunday afternoons entangled upon the three-seater, arguing about which channel to watch, flipping constantly between his news channels, my music channels and inevitably settling on reruns of *Friends*.

But in the meantime, our other furniture purchase attempts also showed the same pattern of strange shopper behaviour on Vijay's part. When it was time to buy a dining table, we found a shop which had a big sale on. Vijay saw one small dining table and chair set that caught his fancy and asked the salesperson how much discount he could get.

The salesperson beamed happily at him and said, 'Sir, this is a great offer. It's actually seventy per cent off.'

Vijay was impressed. 'Seventy per cent, eh?'

The salesperson mistook the question in his voice to be doubt and admitted, 'Well, two of these chairs are just a little chipped near the base – but otherwise, they're in great condition.'

Vijay was inspecting the dining table closely, when suddenly a thought occurred to him. He turned to the salesguy and said accusingly 'Your signs outside say fifty per cent discount.'

The salesguy said, 'Yes, sir …?'

'But you said this has seventy per cent discount?'

'Err … yes …'

Vijay looked at him keenly and said, 'So why does the sign outside not say upto seventy per cent discount?'

The salesguy spluttered. 'Well, yes, sir … you see … there's only this one piece with seventy per cent … so, once it's gone, people will ask why you've put upto seventy per cent … so that's why, sir …'

Vijay seemed satisfied with this explanation and said, 'Hmm. Achha ji. Theek hain ji.' I stood there tapping my feet, wondering what this exchange had to do with anything and why Vijay was making the man feel guilty about a great offer.

This is how I discovered that Vijay had a penchant for irrelevant conversations with strangers, even telecallers. Most people would get annoyed by unsolicited offers, but Vijay saw them as an opportunity to interact with and irritate people. So when someone called with an offer for a credit card, he would grill them for about ten minutes on its costs and benefits before incorrectly informing them that he was a student with no money and no job prospects. They would usually hang up on him and he would then chuckle to himself with quiet satisfaction.

He was even happy when it was a wrong number. I heard him answer one such call with a loud, enthusiastic, 'Oh haanji, haan … You want to speak to Mukesss? … Mukesss not here right now … I'm his brother Suressss … But you give me message, I will give to Mukesss … Mukesss to call you back on this number? … Yess, yess, I will tell him … Anything else, ji? … No ji? … ok ji … Bye bye, ji.' He hung up with an immensely pleased look on his face. When he caught sight of my disapproving face as I stood at the bedroom door, the smile immediately dropped off and he explained seriously, 'Wrong number. Tchah! So irritating.'

During our next shopping excursion, we were attempting to buy a suitcase for my regular work travel. We went to Shopper's Stop and there was an enthusiastic trainee salesboy who was insistent on selling me the suede version of a suitcase that I liked. He told me, 'This colour very good, madam. Suede matrial bahut hi achha rehta hain.' I remarked that this particular light brown colour looked like it would get dirty very soon, so I would prefer the black version. The young man persisted, saying that this color was the most popular. He said he had sold twenty-five pieces already. He then said the wonderful thing about the suede material was that the dirtier it got, the better it looked. He repeated this logic over and over: 'Madam, I'm telling you … Jitna ganda hota hain, aur bhi achha lagta hain,' until Vijay lost his patience and questioned him with exaggerated politeness as to why, if this were true, didn't he just make them even *dirtier* before selling them.

The young trainee had nothing to say in response and looked quite deflated. Out of pity for him, I bought the suitcase, giving my husband a dirty look. The young trainee arranged the billing for us, but he went about it in a rather morose and listless way and it was clear that he was re-evaluating his career options. I didn't blame him.

When it came to blame, I had decided it was always going to be Vijay.

9

Opposites Attack

'So you don't believe in God? At all?' Vijay asked me, the incredulity clear in his voice.

Actually living together as a married couple was proving that my pre-nuptial apprehensions about our differences had not been unfounded. In fact, we clearly had more differences than we had imagined.

We had just finished a late dinner and I stretched and yawned before I got up to clear the table.

'Not really,' I said, as I picked up his plate, put it on top of mine and strode towards the kitchen to put the cutlery in a haphazard pile in the sink. I called over my shoulder, 'Also, I'm not really big on pujas and all that.'

There was a moment of silence, after which he joined me in the kitchen with the rest of the dirty dishes. After carefully balancing his set on the ones I had dumped in the sink, he turned to me and said, 'I kind of like pujas. And we're going to be having a puja every Diwali in Jaipur – you will fold your hands and sing along, right?'

'I suppose I will,' I said. No point in being a rebel without a cause. Then I realized something. 'Wait a minute – we'll have to spend *every* Diwali in Jaipur? Every single year? Never in Delhi with my family?'

'Er, well, yes,' he said. 'It's a family tradition – we all gather there, all of us – it's like we're a joint family for a few days! It's great fun.'

'Vijay, I don't think the idea of a joint family is great fun. I like my space.'

'Yes, but it's just for a few days … and you'll like it – you'll see how bright and colourful Jaipur gets at Diwali, you'll wear nice saris all the time, you'll …'

I almost squeaked in disbelief. 'I'll have to wear saris all the time? You know I hate wearing saris.'

'Er, yes … but you look so good in them. I love saris!'

'Then you wear them, na?'

'I mean, I love women in saris – I mean, I love you in saris.' He saw the look on my face and added, 'I mean, I love you!'

There was a moment of tense silence as we stood there. I registered the sound of running water and noticed that I had left the tap running and the sink was on the brink of overflowing. I sullenly turned the water off and then walked out of the kitchen, back into the living room.

'Come on, it's just a Sharma family thing,' said Vijay as he followed me out.

'Well, fine, but you should just know the Lals do it a bit differently.' I flopped down on the sofa and looked at him.

There was another moment of tense silence.

'Honey,' he said, 'this may not be the best time to ask you this, but you do intend to change your surname from Lal to Sharma, right?'

I thought about it and said, 'No, not really.'

We both looked at each other for a while. Then he gently murmured, 'Perhaps we should have talked a bit more about some of this stuff before marriage.'

I glared at him and said, 'You think?'

There were other contentious issues too, like food.

Vijay didn't like the thought of meat being cooked in the house. Initially I agreed to this, but after braving it out for the first few weeks, I started to crave home-cooked non-veg food and needled him about it occasionally.

'But why can't we cook chicken at home?'

'Because … I am a vegetarian.'

'Vijay, you eat chicken nuggets every time you have beer.'

'That's different,' he protested. 'Chicken nuggets aren't like … chicken,' he finished lamely.

'You also eat egg!'

'But that's also not like chicken – and vegetarians can eat egg!'

'There's a term for this, Vijay …'

'I know! I think it's called ovo-vegetarianism.'

'Well, I was going for "hypocrisy" but sure, whatever works for you.'

After a moment of hurt silence, he said, 'You know, you can be too sarcastic at times.'

'Me, sarcastic? Yeah right.'

'See?'

Then there was also the little matter of his smoking. It was something that drove me up the wall. He was still smoking at least eight to ten cigarettes every day, despite the promise he had made to me before marriage about quitting. I disliked the smell and the smoke intensely but of course, my biggest worry was what it was doing to his health.

I watched him light up yet again after dinner as we sat on the balcony. 'But why, *why* do you have to smoke? It's such a filthy habit.'

He took a long drag and his words came out with a slow, satisfied puff. 'I know. It's terrible.'

'So why don't you keep your promise to quit? You told me you'd quit after marriage.'

'Yes,' he conceded. 'But I didn't specify *when* after marriage! Ha *ha*!'

I glared at him. 'Actually, you said you would quit within the first two months.'

'Oh, did I?' He considered this seriously and then said in a brighter tone, 'In that case, I didn't specify within two months of marrying *you*!'

I gave him one of my most malevolent, withering looks.

He glanced at me, took a quick drag and muttered, 'That look is one of the reasons I may just need to continue.'

I tried to look less withering and cried in despair, 'But *what* do you get out of smoking? What is so important that you would sacrifice your health for it?'

He thought seriously for a minute. 'It helps me focus. And relax.' He gave me a sidelong look which contained a hint of accusation. 'At least it *used* to. Until you started hassling me every time.'

I leaned back in my chair and tried another tack. 'Well,

suit yourself. But do you know research shows that every cigarette makes you lose five minutes of your life?'

He took a long drag, looked at the sky and remarked, 'Is that all? Man ... it is so worth it!'

That did it. I could contain myself no longer. I started sniffing. To his surprise, two fat tears rolled down my cheeks and I declared piteously, 'You're going to die young and leave me all alone and penniless.'

'Hey, hey ... no, no ... don't cry.' He dragged his chair closer to mine and put his arm around me, trying to console me. 'Do you know every time you cry, you lose ten minutes of your life?' I only snorted through my sobs and he continued, 'Seriously ... that's how long on average it takes for you to stop.'

My crying got louder as I realized he still hadn't put out his cigarette.

'And I am not going to die young and leave you alone and penniless.'

I paused to look up hopefully.

'... I'm already paying premiums on this insurance policy from LIC ...'

My bawls rent the stillness of the night.

'Ohhhh no ... Look, look ... I'll show you something ... See? ... Smoke rings!'

And of course, there was the subject of children.

'Honey, my friend Raghu has invited us to his younger son's birthday party,' Vijay said enthusiastically after getting off the phone.

'Okay, have fun then!'

'What? He's invited you too – he couldn't make it to the wedding, so he hasn't even seen you.'

'There's a nice picture of me on the dressing table, take it for him.'

There was a small pause.

'I am getting the feeling,' Vijay said thoughtfully, 'that maybe you don't want to come to the party.'

'I am NOT going to a kiddie birthday party. I can't stand kids.'

Silence filled the space between us.

'You can't? I really like kids – they're so cute.'

'They are monsters.'

'You do realize you were one yourself, right?'

'I was a monster.'

'*Was?*'

I made a face at him and said, 'I just think kids are icky, runny-nosed, loud pests.'

He smiled indulgently. 'I'm sure you're not going to feel that way after we have our first child.'

'Our *what what*?'

'Well, we are going to have children someday soon, right?'

'What are you talking about, Vijay? I'm just twenty-three! I have my whole life ahead of me. I'm not even sure I'll *ever* want a kid.'

'But it would be so nice to have our children running about. Think about it … our own little Pappu and Munni …'

'And that's the other thing – you seem already convinced we're going to have *multiple* children. Do you think childbirth is easy or something? If it's so easy, you do it, na?'

'If I could, I would.' Vijay sighed. 'But nature has planned it this way. Anyway, there's no hurry. Just keep in mind that my biological clock is ticking.'

'Don't be silly, Vijay. You can father children till the age of seventy or something.'

'But all my friends already have children. Raghu has two … There is such a thing as … as…' He struggled for the right words. 'Peer pressure, you know.'

'Well, I'm not having a *baby*' – I spat out the last word – 'just because you feel some strange urge to prove your virility and keep up with the Raghus of this world.'

There was tense silence for a few seconds. Finally Vijay said in an appeasing tone, 'Okay, okay, calm down, I didn't mean to get you so worked up. Let me take you out for a special evening to make it up to you – we'll have a good time and forget all about this silly argument.'

For a moment, I was quite taken with this plan. We had been so busy lately that we hadn't made any time for romantic evenings together and it would be really nice to …

But then a thought struck me and I looked at him carefully and replied, 'Vijay, I'm *not* going to the kiddie birthday party.'

'Oh, all right, forget it then – sit at home only!'

10

The Proud Landowners

'You know what? We should look at putting some money in some land.'

Vijay had been reading the property supplement of the paper while I applied my mind to the cryptic crossword. He folded up his paper with a businesslike rustle and waited for my reaction.

'Really?' I said. I had no idea about these things, but it definitely sounded like the kind of responsible and vaguely boring thing that a married couple would do. 'Cool! What kind of land? How do we go about it?'

For a moment, Vijay looked like he didn't have a clue either. But then he said with determination, 'I'll find out about the options.'

As I had already learnt, nothing made Vijay happier than finding out about the options. This obsessive behaviour applied not just to new purchases or investment decisions – even when he had to choose which socks to wear, he would first check out the options. Basically, he liked having a choice in every matter. Perhaps it made him feel in control. Privately, I put the matter of land completely out of my mind. After all, I reasoned, it had taken us four weeks to buy a sofa. Land would probably take four years.

To my surprise, when we got home that evening, it turned out he had already done some research during the day. 'I got the number of this broker fellow called Dilip and spoke to him – he's showing us a plot of land on Saturday.'

'That was quick,' I said with admiration. 'So what kind of land is it? Will we build a house on it or are we just buying it for investment's sake?'

Vijay could not contain his excitement as he announced, 'It's an agricultural plot in Devanahalli. We're going to *farm* on it!'

Devanahalli was about thirty-five kilometers from the heart of Bangalore, basically in the middle of nowhere. I waited a moment to see if he was joking, but it didn't look like it. His smile turned dreamy as he continued, 'I've always wanted to own a piece of land on which I could grow my own stuff. Maybe even eventually make a living out of it by growing some medicinal crops, there's a lot of money to be made in those. And the fresh air and the feeling of being close to nature – wah!'

He was saying something about vanilla, amla and something that sounded like Jethro Tull to me, but turned out to be jatropha. My mind was wandering a bit. I liked Nature as much as the next girl, but had never seen myself as a farmer's wife. Out loud, I said, 'Achha, that's all very nice. But don't you think we should perhaps look at something more practical? As in, maybe buy some land and sell it for a profit so that we can get our own flat or something?'

Then I noticed Vijay's expression. He looked like somebody had punctured all his tyres, including the spare, and so I continued quickly, 'But there's no harm in checking it out, right? Just as an option.'

Vijay was happy again and I thought maybe it actually wouldn't be such a bad idea to own some land near Bangalore. The busy corporate couple that we were, it could be our weekend sanctuary. A place where we could perhaps even entertain good friends. Get away from the madness of the city for a couple of days of rustic rest and relaxation.

Saturday rolled around and the two of us got ready bright and early. We were meeting the broker Dilip in the city and then driving together to the land.

It was a beautiful morning. The weather was pleasant and mild and there was a cool breeze. We drove with the windows down, enjoying the fact that we were putting some distance between us and the pollution and chaos of the city. The drive was long but the view was scenic and Dilip was a quiet, honest-looking sort of chap who struck me as the antithesis of the loud, obnoxious type that I had thought a broker should ideally be.

He spoke only a little, to tell us a bit more about the land. It seemed that it was owned by a family in Bangalore, who had been unable to spend time and money in cultivating it and now wanted to buy some land closer to the city. According to Dilip, they wanted to get rid of it at a throwaway price of five and a half lakh rupees. This still sounded like quite a bit of money to me so I firmly resolved that there would be negotiations – if we liked the land at all, of course.

With Dilip's directions, we finally got to the land. It was quite far from the main road and we had to travel on a dirt track for about a kilometre, which Vijay noted with a muttered 'Bad approach road' as he struggled with the wheel to stay on the track. Finally, in a cloud of dust, we pulled up in front of the gate of the plot.

We got out, stretched and looked around appraisingly. The plot was fenced off, in the middle of a fairly barren stretch of land. As we walked through the gate, we were greeted by an old Kannadiga couple who served as the caretakers.

The place itself was beautiful. It was running a bit wild here and there but it seemed to be teeming with all sorts of vegetation. It was segregated into different parts and to my delight, one portion had mango trees. Vijay walked around with Dilip and the caretaker and carefully checked the various crops. There was a vegetable patch with potatoes, cauliflower, tomatoes and so on. I had a feeling Vijay was already imagining the taste of his all-time favourite dish – alu gobi – cultivated from scratch.

The land was also much larger than I had imagined. I asked Dilip about the size and he said it was ten acres. It was so large that I stopped following Vijay around after a while and just sat down on a tree stump.

It was quiet and peaceful. The cool breeze brought with it scents of the different plants and trees. The only constant sound was the buzzing of insects. There were also a cow and a few goats owned by the caretakers which, I thought approvingly, gave the place just the right sort of rustic touch. It was intoxicating.

The clincher for us, especially as far as Vijay was concerned, was the borewell. It was not very well maintained, as Dilip admitted, but with some work, it could supply almost all the water required for the irrigation of the land. Vijay was fascinated by the borewell, insisting on drinking its water from it because the caretaker told him it was very sweet. I protested, afraid that he might keel over clutching his throat and die on the spot, or perhaps less dramatically, develop a stomach bug – but he simply cupped his hands and downed a mouthful of the water, leaned back to savour it and pronounced it indeed the sweetest water that he had ever tasted. His exact words were, 'Wah!'

I observed him as he sat crosslegged next to the borewell. The white kurta that he had donned for the visit made him look like some sort of benign, mild-mannered young thakur. He asked the caretaker all sorts of questions about the different types of soils on the land, discussed with him and Dilip the merits and demerits of the various crops, which had thrived and which had not, and even held forth on what, in his opinion, the owners could have done differently. They had an extended conversation and the caretaker's wife then served us steaming tea in steel glasses that were so hot that they were a challenge to hold. 'Made with goat's milk,' she said in Kannada and Dilip translated for us. We were a bit sceptical about how it would taste, but after a sip or two, we were pleasantly surprised.

Dilip asked us what we thought, and Vijay and I looked at each other. I gave him a smooth, almost imperceptible nod. He missed it and continued to look blankly at my face for my reaction. I pulled him aside and hissed, 'It's nice. But *negotiate*.'

Vijay nodded and we went back to Dilip. Vijay said that we were prepared to look at the land, but only for five lakh rupees. Dilip said that five and a half lakh was already a very low price and that we could ask anyone about it. But he would try and convince the landowners to consider this price for us because he thought we were a very nice couple and he hadn't seen any of the other prospective buyers take such an interest in the different aspects of the land as Vijay had. We also seemed to have the blessings of the caretaker and his wife, as they stood around eavesdropping blatantly, with ingratiating toothless grins. We shook hands with Dilip solemnly and left, thanking the caretakers for their hospitality.

We were now very excited about the prospect of owning the land. It was a fair amount of money for us, because I had just started work and Vijay had not felt the need to save a single paisa of his earnings till now. But we were certain we would be able to arrange it through some means – maybe a loan.

When we got home that evening, we talked about the various things that we would do with the land, maybe construct a little farmhouse on it over time or even a small guest house, eventually developing it into a resort. Vijay started off on his agricultural plan, but I tuned out again somewhere around jatropha and instead closed my eyes and imagined indulging myself in the jacuzzi of my very own spa-resort, while he rambled on happily about the various crop options.

By the time Monday rolled around, we were convinced that Dilip would have swung the deal for us and that we now fell in the category of landed gentry. In fact, as we discussed it on the way to work, we recklessly said we would be prepared to pay fifty thousand rupees more for the land, if it came to that. In the office, we talked about it with a few people and they seemed quite impressed, saying that five lakh rupees did sound like a throwaway price for ten acres – in fact, they warned us to be very careful because the price appeared to be so low that perhaps there was something wrong with the ownership of the land. We scoffed at them, saying that of course we would ensure we checked everything out carefully with the help of a lawyer. After all, it wasn't like we were stupid.

That evening, Vijay got a breathless call from Dilip. 'Sir, they are close to getting an offer for five point five lakh. I am telling them that if you pay even five point two, you are the people they should sell to – is five point two lakh okay?'

Vijay was very capable of making quick decisions on the spot. 'Dilip, I'm not even discussing this with my wife. Just go ahead and tell them that five point two is fine for us.'

'Great, sir. I will call you back in one hour.' Dilip hung up.

Vijay looked over at me and nodded. He held out his hand and I high-fived it.

When Dilip called back, Vijay put him on speaker phone.

'Sir, they've agreed. Can we set up a meeting tomorrow evening, five p.m., at their residence in Koramangla?'

'That sounds fine,' said Vijay. 'Thanks a lot, Dilip.'

'It's okay, sir,' said Dilip modestly. 'It's a good deal, sir.

Getting an all-white deal for fifty-two lakh rupees is not easy nowadays.'

His voice was all amplified and tinny and his words seemed to echo in the ensuing silence.

Vijay attempted to keep his voice level. 'What did you say, Dilip?'

'Sir, all-white deal for fifty-two lakh is not at all easy ...'

'*Fifty-two lakh* rupees?' Vijay's expression as he looked at me was a mask of horror. I was sure mine mirrored it.

Dilip went on to say something else, but I had stopped listening. It all fell into place now. He had always said five point two lakh – of *course* he had meant five point two lakh per *acre*. I decided this was Vijay's fault, as usual. He was the one who had started the entire discussion with Dilip. He should have been more careful. He should have been more aware. He should have ...

Vijay was saying, 'Er, Dilip, you know what? We may need to get back to you on this.'

Dilip was taken aback, 'But sir ... the meeting tomorrow?'

Vijay said, 'Okay bye' and hung up.

We stared at each other wordlessly, and then the expressions of horror faded as helpless laughter took over instead. Vijay pointed at me and laughed. 'And you thought five point two lakh rupees was too high ... ha ha ha!'

I retaliated by mocking him. 'What about you? Drinking the water from the borewell, sitting there like some sort of thakur ... Haan, yeh paani toh bahut meetha hain ... Wah!'

'Poor Dilip,' he said once the laughter had passed. We maintained a respectful silence for him for a minute. Then Vijay asked me, 'So exactly how do you plan to explain this to him?' He deftly ducked out of the way to avoid the pillow I threw.

Poor Dilip was quite disappointed when Vijay finally called him to explain why we were backing out of the deal. Vijay said that we had consulted with some legal experts and there were apparently quite a few issues with the registration for ownership of agricultural land, especially in Karnataka, and it was not a hassle that we were willing to take on at the moment. He also added that we had decided we needed to be a bit more practical and purchase a flat before thinking about any other large investments. He thanked him for his efforts and apologized for the wasted time.

Dilip, who seemed to epitomize the expression Nice Guys Finish Last, said that he understood and respected our decision. He also agreed that the registration issue was a real problem in Karnataka if you didn't happen to be originally from the state and said it was wise of Vijay to have found out about it. Of course, said Vijay smugly, it was our investment, so we had to look at it from all angles.

After all, it wasn't like we were stupid.

11

Driving Miss Crazy

It was a pleasantly dull Sunday morning when Vijay turned to me and remarked, 'I think it's time you learned to drive.'

'*Or*,' I suggested, 'we could get a driver?'

'Ya, sure! Or *maybe*,' said Vijay, 'you could just learn to drive?'

Vijay had been dutifully transporting me from place to place during the last few months, but he was getting tired of it now. I noticed a lot of the things that he had been willing to do when we were not yet married, he was trying to sidle out of now. I decided to confront him with this.

'How come you were happy to drive me around earlier, but now have a problem with it?'

He stretched lazily and yawned. He then told me, 'Ab toh ladki phassa di, na? Ab kyon mehnat karoon?'

'Aha!' I cried. 'This is just like the smoking. You *promised* you would quit before we got married and then ...'

'Hai rabba, not that again,' Vijay said in a panicked voice. 'Didn't *you* promise you would use that only once a week, the last time we fought?'

I was silent.

Thus began my driving lessons.

I remembered with some trepidation the driving lessons I had taken while in college, back in Delhi. I had been a mere eighteen-year-old, hopeful and sunny. There was a bored looking instructor who would come by every day with a beat-up old Maruti 800, to give me a half-hour lesson in negotiating the deathtraps otherwise known as the roads of Delhi. The most important feature of these driving-school vehicles was the extra set of brakes on the passenger side, which the instructor, when startled out of his boredom by a bad move on my part, would stomp on, bringing the car to a grinding halt.

Driving was complicated. There were multiple gears, switches and nothing was labelled properly. When asked to 'give the right indicator', I would turn on the windshield wipers. While attempting to turn them off, I would switch the lights on to high beam. I would start to panic and it would all be downhill from there. I could rarely get anything right and my instructor's boredom had a tinge of disgust added to it by the end of each lesson.

There was one day that stood out very clearly in my memory – the day of my near-death experience. Okay, it was not really *my* near-death experience, but that of a silly cow that had plonked itself right in my way. I was speeding along a straight road, no traffic in sight for a change, and this dumb bovine sat in thoughtful repose right in my path. Irritated, I honked and honked but it just did not move. We were almost on top of the thoughtless animal when my bored instructor suddenly snapped out of his reverie and yelled 'BRAKE!' In the panic, I promptly pressed the accelerator, but the action was thankfully overridden by my instructor stepping on the brakes on his side with all his weight. The car screeched to a halt inches from the cow who, apparently affronted by this intrusion into her personal space, got up and sauntered away after one condescending look at me.

My instructor was looking at me in disbelief and I pre-empted him with 'I kept blowing the horn, but that cow just didn't move … what could I do?'

I thought I heard his teeth grinding as he said, 'Why didn't you just slow down?'

There was absolutely no logical answer to this. I decided to go on the offensive and said, 'Why didn't *you* tell me to slow down? You're the instructor.'

Faced with this regrettable but undeniable truth, the instructor leaned back in his seat and growled, 'Start the car.'

We drove in silence. I was tempted to remind him that I had definitely improved since the previous week, when instead of slowing down while approaching a speed bump, I had honked repeatedly at it, as if I expected it to flatten itself out or move elsewhere by the time I reached it. The instructor had been disgusted with me that day too. Safer not to bring it up.

There was an intersection coming up where we had to take a right turn and this time I was determined to impress the man by doing it just right. I carefully re-adjusted my mirror to the precise angle in order to gauge the traffic behind me. Well in time, I switched on the indicator to show the other drivers behind me that I was planning to turn to the right. As I approached the intersection, I released the accelerator gently and pressed the brake, slowing to just the right speed. I smoothly changed the gear from third to second. And I didn't even stall the car!

I had carried out the whole operation within a matter of seconds without a single mistake and without even breaking into a sweat. I grinned triumphantly at my instructor, expecting to hear the praise I rightfully deserved.

'Very nice,' he remarked sardonically. 'But you forgot to *take the right turn!*'

I was sullen for the rest of the drive home, feeling discouraged. I discontinued my classes soon after that day. Possibly, the driving instructor discontinued his career soon after, too. I would have if I were him. Thankless job, really.

So I really could not be blamed for the trepidation I felt now, as I took my place behind the wheel after so many years of having successfully avoided it. Vijay tried to calm me down, saying it would be just fine and it was just a matter of my developing a little confidence.

He guided me through the basics. 'Okay, just adjust the seat to a comfortable position ... your legs are very short ... I mean compared to mine, of course ... Is the mirror okay? ... No, stop checking your own face in it, you look fine ... Now, remember ... this is ...'

'I know, I remember,' I said with a touch of excitement as I pointed them out. 'A-B-C … Accelerator … Brake … Clutch.'

'Very good,' said Vijay, but uncertainty was creeping into his voice. 'Except that it's right-to-left and not left-to-right. That's kind of important.'

'Oh yeah, you're right. I remember now,' I said and gulped.

'What's wrong?'

I took a deep breath and tried to fight the panic rising in my throat. 'It's just that … I just noticed this car doesn't have a brake on the passenger side …'

'It will be fine,' he said soothingly. 'Let's go.'

That was my cue to show him my stuff and I instinctively fiddled with a few things to start the car. To my surprise, I remembered how to do it – apparently it was like riding a bicycle, you never forget it.

So I revved up the engine and off we went – for about two seconds before I stalled the car. I kept trying, but somehow I just could not ease my foot off the clutch smoothly enough and the car kept stalling.

'Ha ha,' I said, my voice catching. 'Little rusty.'

I tried once more and failed. In frustration, I remarked, 'This is difficult. Not just anyone can do it. They should have a test.'

'They do,' he reminded me. Something occurred to him. 'Hey, just how did you pass your test? You have a valid driver's license, right?'

'Oh yes,' I said. 'I passed my test because in the written part, they asked a series of questions on road signs and traffic rules and I had mugged it all up very nicely. Then they just made me drive forwards and backwards … yes, I know it's called reverse … and I somehow managed it that day.' My voice became defensive, 'I *can* drive a little, you know, it's just that I'm out of practice now.'

'And practice is what you're going to get,' he said with determination. 'Try again.'

Eventually, I managed to get the car going again and powered by a series of small jerks, we moved towards the main road.

'I'm driving!' I said with glee.

Vijay was all business. 'Look at the road.'

I snapped back to attention.

When we reached the main road, I stopped.

'What are you doing?' he asked. 'The road is all clear.'

'I'm not going out there,' I cried. 'There's *traffic* on this road.'

'Honey, the only way you'll get comfortable driving is by getting used to traffic. Come on, take a right turn here, let's go to Indira Nagar.'

Muttering that he would regret this, I did what he said. We somehow managed to make it to the intersection just before Indira Nagar when suddenly the memory of failing to take the turn at the intersection during my driving lessons hit me, just like a flashback from a Hindi movie. I broke into a cold sweat and prayed fervently that I would not stall the car. Anything but stalling the car.

I stalled the car.

Within five seconds, what felt like all the vehicles in Bangalore were bearing down on us, honking angrily. I was glued to my seat, looking around dumbly, unable to move. Vijay was saying something in an urgent tone to me, but I couldn't hear him. The icing on my panic attack was the fact that an angry traffic cop was now approaching. Before he could start shouting at me, Vijay opened his door and stood up with one foot still inside the car, explaining to him that I was just learning. The traffic cop said that I should go and learn somewhere else and Vijay said we were just going.

I regained my senses and started the car and eased it forward smoothly. The little detail that I did not take into account was that my husband was still in conversation with the angry cop, and half of him – head, shoulders and one leg – was still outside the car. He was hanging on to the car door for dear life as he found himself suddenly being dragged along in this awkward position. I only braked when I became aware of his panicked screams. I looked at his face as he bent down to glare at me, his expression shocked and disbelieving. I gathered he would live and tried to make up for my little boo-boo by giving him a winning smile. It didn't work.

'Move over,' he barked at me. 'I'm going to drive.' He detached himself from the car door. Something seemed to occur to him and he hissed at me, 'Do *not* drive over me. Touch *nothing*.'

Just to be safe, he circled over to my side from the rear of the car. I dully moved over to the passenger side. The cacophony of honks and angry shouts outside had reached near-deafening levels, but I was now only aware of the fact that I had nearly killed my husband. Completely unintentionally. And so soon after marriage, too.

'So … are we getting a driver?' I ventured later that evening, after a nice cup of tea had calmed us both down.

'No,' said Vijay decidedly. 'I'm going to teach you, even if it kills me.'

I wisely kept to myself the thought that *that* was no longer just a figure of speech, but assented to further driving lessons, figuring that nothing could be worse than today.

To my surprise, over the next few weeks of sustained practice under his watchful guidance and terse instructions, I actually became comfortable with driving.

After a couple of months, I began to consider myself a bit of a pro. Vijay did not seem to concur, often snapping at me, 'Did you see that car coming up in the rearview mirror?' or 'Did you notice that pothole you barely avoided?'

I always snapped back, 'Of course, what do you think?' But I was usually lying.

I even began to drive myself to office and back whenever Vijay was out of town. In fact, were it not for the fact that I had absolutely no sense of direction, I would have driven myself everywhere I wanted to go.

12

The Ladies' Man

'Did I ever tell you about my school and college girlfriends?' Vijay asked, a faraway, wistful look on his face.

'Yes, Vijay,' I rolled my eyes. 'Several times. There were only like, three, you know.'

Vijay hadn't had too much success with romance in his early years. He related these tragic stories to me in the clear hope of arousing some sympathy, but it was the comic side that shone through for me.

Enemy no. 1 of his attempts at romance was his older sister Shyama didi, who nipped the first of these cruelly in the bud.

At the tender age of fifteen, Vijay was delighted one day to note that they had new neighbours and one of the daughters of the new-family-on-the-block was his age. She was fifteen, she was a girl and she was next door – three things that qualified her immediately for the perfect and natural choice for his first romance.

Vijay spent unusual amounts of time each day hanging around in his garden, hoping to start a conversation over the fence. He was eventually successful and the young girl Bindu was quite taken with the gangly youth that Vijay was. They struck up a firm friendship over the fence.

Of course, Vijay had to be careful that no one from his conservative family got wind of this relationship. He thus enlisted his friend Dhruv to play the part of Lookout. While Vijay whispered sweet nothings to blushing Bindu, Dhruv lurked in the background keeping an eye on the house so that if someone came out, Vijay could be adequately warned.

It would have been better perhaps if they had established beforehand what they would actually do in case such a situation arose. One day, as Vijay was romancing his lady love, Dhruv spotted Vijay's mother, ubiquitously called Mummy by everyone who knew her, coming out of the house. Dhruv panicked and started jumping up and down, shouting, 'Mummyyy … Mummyyy …' in a nervous, high-pitched voice. Vijay and Bindu stopped talking and stared at Dhruv as he pranced around the garden, giving the distinct impression that he was suddenly pining for his mother. It was lucky that Mummyji herself stopped in her tracks at the doorway, sufficiently distracted by this spectacle, giving Vijay enough time to put some distance between himself and his young love and pretend to be studiously examining the leaves on some plants instead. Mummy remarked later at dinner that perhaps Dhruv was not quite all right in the head and suggested Vijay make some new friends.

The romance, alas, was doomed in any case. One day, Vijay made the mistake of putting his feelings on paper in the form of a love letter for Bindu. When Shyama didi entered his room, she was curious to see what he was writing, since Vijay was never spotted at his books outside of school. She asked him what he was doing and he refused to answer her. When she made a grab for the letter, an indignant Vijay ran out of the room with it. Realizing that she was determinedly giving chase, he ducked out the front door, tore the letter into tiny pieces and threw them beyond the garden fence. He then gave his sister a triumphant look before walking off – he would have to recompose his letter but he had at least shown Shyama didi that it didn't pay to interfere with his life.

Shyama didi showed a great deal of patience and dedication in this matter. She went about assiduously gathering as many of the pieces of the torn paper as she could find and then painstakingly put them together like a jigsaw puzzle, using cellotape as an aid. Once she had read enough of the letter to confirm her suspicions, she lay in wait for him. Since she was eight years older than Vijay and protective of him, she felt it was only right for her to give him what was coming.

And what was coming to poor hapless Vijay was one of the most resounding slaps across the face that he had ever received in his life.

As he stood in numb silence in their living room, holding his reddening cheek with the echo of the slap still bouncing off the walls, Mummyji came in and asked them what on earth was going on. Shyama didi was too loyal to rat on Vijay and didn't want to scandalize their pious Mummyji with the nefarious deeds of her son, so the two of them just stood there mumbling and looking at their feet and the matter was eventually let go. As was poor, innocent, heartbroken Bindu.

It was in college that Vijay met his second girlfriend – a girl called Vidya.

Vijay studied, if the term is used in the loosest possible sense, at the illustrious IIT-Delhi. Most of the students at this institute were males whose sole means of interacting with members of the opposite sex was through the 'Social' – an eagerly awaited event where girls from other colleges would be invited for a dance party. Vidya from Jesus and Mary College made her appearance at one such event.

Vijay, or Lambu as he was nicknamed at IIT, was a position holder – he was a house secretary – and therefore one of the haves in the college hierarchy; he was over six feet tall and had longish hair swept along his forehead in the style of the day's Hindi film heroes. So you could say he was amongst the more desirable specimens at IIT, although perhaps that still wasn't saying very much.

Vidya seemed to like him and after some foot-shuffling on his part and some eyelash-batting on hers, they got to talking and even had a couple of dances together.

Over the next few months, their relationship blossomed through the exchange of frequent cards and letters. Without Shyama didi hovering over his shoulder, Vijay was able to express himself freely and romantically and they looked forward to their meeting at the next Social.

The evening of the party, Vijay stood around with his friends, waiting for the bus with the girls from JMC to arrive. When the bus finally pulled up and the girls piled out, there was a moment of shy uncertainty as both groups eyed each other expectantly. Then the girls giggled and started to enter the hall in bunches of two and three.

Vijay's friend Vishal, or Mota as he was fondly called, leaned over to him and said, 'So, Lambu? Which one is your girl?'

He got no answer and looked up to see Lambu's face all scrunched up in confusion. Vijay finally let out a chagrined 'I don't know! They all look the same to me.'

'What? You can't recognize your own girlfriend?'

'I met her only once!'

Mota nodded slowly in sympathy and said, 'Lambu. Ek baat bolu? Tu bahut bada ch**iya hain.'

At this point, one of the giggling girls passing by paused to give Vijay a meaningful smile and then continued on her way. 'That was her!' said Vijay.

Mota was relieved but asked, 'Are you sure?'

'No. But she smiled at me, so I'll try her first.'

It turned out that the smiling girl was indeed Vidya. However, the realization that she hadn't left enough of an impression for him to even remember her face made Vijay feel that she was not destined to be the love of his life. He soon found himself getting bored and listless with her chatter and longed to join his gang of buddies, who were now huddled together in a drunk circle, poking fun at all the people on the dance floor.

In desperation, he broke away from her for a few minutes and went rummaging behind the speakers. Sure enough, he found what he was looking for – a half-full bottle of vodka. Throwing caution to the winds, he consumed its entire contents and emerged, as often happens under the influence of alcohol, a changed person.

He weaved his way back to Vidya in a debonair manner,

only tripping once at the end of the journey and almost knocking her over. She was suddenly overwhelmed by the smell of alcohol and said pettishly, 'You know, Vijay? I think there is someone who may be drinking here!'

He leaned in close, towering over her. 'Really? How do you know?'

She leaned back warily. 'I can smell it …'

'Oh, is that so?' he said, leaning in even closer. Without warning, he suddenly exhaled in a loud huff, all over her face. 'Quick – can you smell it on my breath?'

Her face all screwed up and holding her own breath, she responded with a scared and automatic, 'No'.

'Well then, in that case, no one is drinking here. So let usss enjoyyy!' He leered at her and started contorting his long limbs in drunk, hypnotic dance movements. She backed away from him in alarm.

That was the end of Vijay's relationship with Vidya. She backed straight into the arms of another young man from IIT named Vikram. They spent the evening together discussing the many character flaws of Vijay Sharma. She sobbed, 'I don't know what happened, he was such a gentleman before.' Vikram growled protectively, something along the lines of 'That b*****d Lambu is a total ch**. Er, what I mean is, a lovely girl like you is too good for someone like him.' A few years later, they were married and Vijay proudly took full credit for their happiness – even though neither ever spoke to him again.

In his final year, Vijay met a gentle young aspiring doctor from Maulana Azad Medical College – Sania. They spent a lovely Delhi summer together and the fact that he didn't once forget what her face looked like was proof of the fact that she meant something special to him.

However, while the Hindu-Muslim thing meant damn-all to the young lovers, Sania's father had a different point of view. One day, he found out about the two of them through an ill-concealed photograph in one of his daughter's books and within a short time, the entire family was gone without a trace.

Vijay's heart was truly broken this time and he moped about in Jaipur for many weeks after his graduation. It was to offer him some much-needed counsel that his good friend Dhruv – the selfsame Dhruv of the earlier 'Mummy-Mummy' fame – wrote him a heartfelt letter.

In Vijay's family, the concept of privacy had apparently not yet been invented. If a letter arrived for any one of them, whoever first saw it would typically tear it open and read it. It so happened that the day Dhruv's letter arrived, Vijay was out and it was received by Papaji. He and Mummyji were the ones to consume its inflammatory and unpalatable contents. For Dhruv, who apparently liked to take, or at least recommend the more decisive and dramatic courses of possible action, had exhorted Vijay in the letter to 'not let religious divides between Hindus and Muslims stand in the way of his happiness' and to 'find her and then elope at the earliest possible with his true love.'

When Vijay came home, his parents had a thing or two to say to him and they said it well into the night. By the time morning came around, he had reconciled to the fact that perhaps he and Sania were not meant to be in this particular lifetime, although he would always continue to hold her in the highest esteem.

Dhruv's esteem with Mummyji, however, dropped to rock bottom levels. As always, she was welcoming and polite, but she began referring to him in conversation with Vijay as 'Woh tera bawla dost.'

As much as I was amused by the stories of Vijay's past loves, I found myself also feeling resentful of the wistfulness with which he mentioned them – perhaps it was the fact that he described all of them as very sweet and gentle girls, which was, I suspected in moments of honest introspection, probably not how most people would choose to describe me. If they did, they had always kept it a very well-guarded secret.

Our temperaments really were so different. Once again, I found myself feeling apprehensive that these differences would lead to serious problems in the future.

Only time would tell.

13

Of Chai in Jaipur

We hadn't been to Jaipur since the wedding, so we decided to go there for a couple of days to spend time with Mummyji and Papaji. Part of me looked forward to the trip wherein I would get to be the bahu, but most of me was filled with trepidation, since it was obvious that I would really have to work hard in order to fit in.

I was still thinking about this as we pulled up in the taxi at their house. During our previous visit, I had watched Garima at our common in-laws' place. She would wake up at 6 a.m., deftly don a sari, go into the kitchen and help Mummyji with all the cooking and generally behave like a good daughter-in-law. She had the advantage of more years in the family and of course, a similar upbringing in a family from a similar background, in nearby Ajmer. Clearly, she had set the precedent for the younger bahu, namely moi. 'Traitor,' I thought malevolently as the door opened.

Mummyji and Papaji were delighted to see us. I murmured something as I touched their feet – I was still embarrassed and shy around them. Mummyji looked at me keenly and declared that I was looking very tired and it was understandable, considering how hard I worked and that the flight from Bangalore was probably not very comfortable and that it was a very hectic schedule that I had and so on and how I should probably go and have a little rest right away. I let myself be ushered into our room, gladly escaping the action for a while to compose myself. It was only 9 p.m., so I thought I would lie down for a few minutes while Vijay spoke to his parents. The next thing I knew, it was morning already.

I hissed at Vijay, who was lying next to me, 'Vijay! Why didn't you wake me up last night?'

He mumbled, 'What? Oh … we thought you were really tired and …' Before completing his explanation, he was asleep again, his mouth and one eye half-open.

I looked around the room and noticed with a start that it was already 8.30 a.m. And here I had been planning to wake up early and help in the kitchen. I wondered what to do next. By this time, Mummyji had probably been up for the last three hours, having had her bath, done her puja, prepared the tea, cooked a delicious breakfast and accomplished other sundry chores.

Feeling somewhat guilty, I thought I would at least make some cosmetic changes, so I went in for a bath, glad that the common bathroom was free. When I was done, I sneaked out and darted back to our room and started to attempt to put on a sari. After about thirty minutes of this – with only a few minutes of pretending it was my Superwoman cape – it was still hanging loose and inadequate about my person.

I prodded Vijay awake again. He was the self-proclaimed sari expert and had promised to help me with it. I barked at him that it was time to make good. He stretched good-naturedly and sat up in bed, looking at my attempt so far. A smile came over his face and he proceeded to explain, correct and help. To my surprise, he actually knew what he was talking about. It escaped me as to how and why he had learned this art. Still, thanks to him, I finally emerged from our room looking the radiant but demure young bride.

Mummyji greeted me enthusiastically and exhorted me to have my tea and drink some milk. I didn't quite know how to manage both. Now that the ordeal of tying the sari was over, I started feeling unoccupied and useless. I walked into the kitchen, remembering just in the nick of time to remove my slippers outside the door. I stood next to Mummyji, who was humming to herself blissfully as she stirred some sabzis. Breakfast having been already prepared, she had immediately started the lunch and dinner preparations.

I noted how she made everything lovingly and painstakingly from scratch – absolutely no short cuts. I already knew from Vijay's descriptions how every single dish that emerged from her kitchen was a treat – whether it was alu ka parathas, dal-baati, meethe chawal, namkeen chawal, atte ka halwa, chakli or Vijay's favourite, alu gobi. Despite a little competition from her flower garden, it was her kitchen that was her true pride and joy.

I vaguely thought that by hanging around while she

cooked I would somehow be helping her and also learning how to cook, perhaps by osmosis – but neither seemed to be happening. While we chatted, mostly about what their many relatives in Jaipur were doing, I kept losing interest in the actual cooking and idly wondering how amazing it was that she could stand for hours at the stove without a break when my own knees already felt like they would give way any minute.

At lunchtime, I insisted upon making the rotis. I was eager to demonstrate my newfound skill. I finally served my attractively misshapen creations, including one nearly perfect rhombus, with pride. I received many wah-wahs for the effort and stood beaming at the family while they all forced my rotis down. But later at dinner, when I announced that I would make rotis again, there was an almost unanimous and emphatic chorus of 'no's. Mummyji quickly added that I must be so tired after so many days of work and on this little break, I should just rest.

I was determined to help, though. I decided that the least I could do was lay the table for dinner and so I happily pottered around back and forth between the kitchen and the table, with all the plates, forks, spoons, katoris and glasses I could manage to find and laid them all out in a pretty and thoughtful pattern. I surveyed my work with satisfaction and then went off to my room for a while. When I came back, the glasses had been replaced by steel tumblers, the plain steel plates had been replaced by ones with patterns, the forks had apparently been deemed redundant, the spoons I had selected were apparently too small and had been replaced by bigger ones. I looked around dismally, and was only slightly cheered to find that the katoris I had selected were still in place. Just then, Mummyji pottered in with a set of four small katoris and as I watched, she replaced my katoris, explaining that they were too big for the dal and why didn't I just go have a little rest.

After much thought on the subject, I hit upon a role that I could play faultlessly on a regular basis – as the official tea-maker. This would be my thing, my niche. One of the first things Vijay had taught me to make was tea. Besides, I had now been working in marketing for a tea brand for months. Consequently, I fancied myself something of a tea expert. From the next day onwards, I started lurking in the darker corridors of the house, pouncing on whoever passed by and offering to make them tea – nay, insisting on it.

This usually turned out to be the hapless Papaji, who (till now) had not been a heavy drinker of tea. But I plied him with cup after cup on the slightest excuse, convincing him each time on different grounds – it was good for digestion, it contained theanine that helped in focused relaxation, it contained antioxidants and only about half the amount of caffeine as coffee – which he never touched, anyway. This kept me reasonably busy over the next three days and I achieved a considerable degree of success with this initiative, despite the little handicap that for some reason, while pouring it out, I tended to spill about as much tea as I made. I countered this problem with a logical and intelligent solution – I simply started to make twice the required quantity. I had an MBA, after all.

On the fourth afternoon, I was doing my thing with the tea, making some for everybody, while Mummyji sat in the drawing room with Vijay and Papaji. The tea took me about twenty minutes to prepare. I heated the water, adding copious amounts of ginger, cardamom and even a little cinnamon. I then added just the right amount of sugar, and brought it to a boil. I lowered the flame on the gas and added four loving pinches of my very own brand of tea powder, which I had insisted replace the erstwhile household favourite. After a couple of minutes of letting it simmer, I added the milk and let it boil over again. I carefully poured out four cups, wiped up the copious spillage and brought the steaming tea out on a tray. The others took their cups and I sat down with them. I took a sip from my own cup with a sigh of satisfaction. It tasted perfect – and there was really nothing like tea prepared from scratch for these precious moments with the family. 'Very nice chai,' said Papaji encouragingly and Vijay and Mummyji murmured in agreement. Mummyji, clearly unable to sit still as usual, soon got up to potter about in the kitchen.

It suddenly struck me that I'd better check whether I had switched off the gas, since this was a tiny detail that sometimes escaped me. I went into the kitchen and found I had indeed switched it off this time. I also found Mummyji standing there, with her back to me, pouring more milk into the cup of tea I had made for her. As I watched, she also added one heaped teaspoon of sugar and started stirring. She was unaware of my presence and was humming to herself happily what sounded like a particularly peppy bhajan for Krishna bhagwan. I left her to it and wordlessly exited the kitchen, feeling a little despondent.

While Vijay's parents appeared to be convinced that I was Loser No. 1 when it came to household matters, they were very proud of the fact that I had a career. I did my best to convince them that I was just a lowly brand manager – mere flotsam in the corporate food chain – but they didn't seem to get it.

I was thus introduced as 'Itni badi company ki bahut badi

officer' to a duly impressed Chauhan uncle, who visited the day before we were due to return to Bangalore. Chauhan uncle was an old friend of the family, who came by with his 'Missus' for a cup of tea one evening. In keeping with the charming practice that still prevailed in the older circles in Jaipur, they dropped in unannounced.

We all sat around in the drawing room, chatting and exchanging pleasantries. I was blissfully absorbed in the conversation, although I didn't participate much and was in actuality fascinated by and secretly keeping track of the number of times the phrase 'Aur, aap kaise hain?' was used. Mummyji got up shortly after, presumably to prepare the tea, which I generously and distractedly left to her this time round. After a while, Papaji made an exit as well. This left me and Vijay to hold the fort; Chauhan uncle and he chatted about this and that and the Missus and I kept smiling at each other, unable to find any common ground until I had a brainwave and asked her in a friendly manner, 'Aur, aap kaise hain?' Thankfully we were soon rejoined by Mummyji and the conversation moved on to other things.

After a few minutes, I noticed Papaji discreetly calling me out of the room. I followed him curiously and saw that he had carefully put together a large tray with assorted namkeen, biscuits and steaming cups of Mummyji's tea. He asked me to take it out to the drawing room and I said 'Of course' and started to carry it out.

Before I could lift the tray, he suggested that I should perhaps wait a few more minutes before doing so. I agreed to this too, vaguely wondering why this was necessary. Then the realization hit me that waiting a while before entering the room would make it look like I had put everything together myself, as a good bahu would probably have done in these parts. I grinned at Papaji conspiratorially and had it been anyone else, would probably also have winked and given the thumbs-up sign. He smiled back a little wistfully and then went off into the drawing room. I timed myself for exactly four and a half minutes by the clock and entered the living room demurely with the tray, to the clear satisfaction of all the observers in the room.

Only Vijay had a wry, knowing smile on his face.

14

Of Alu Gobi in Delhi

On the way back from Jaipur, we were going to spend a couple of days at my mother's place in Delhi before heading back home to Bangalore. I was pretty sure that while I had admirably played the part of square peg to the bahu-shaped hole in Vijay's family, he was going to simply ease into mine with the smoothness of a hand slipping into a well-worn glove.

My mother had already become especially fond of him – in fact, from the first meeting itself. After our wedding, I had remarked to someone that Vijay was clearly going to be like the 'son that my mother never had'. Unfortunately, my brother Abhimanyu had been hovering within earshot and had come up to me with an indignant 'Hello?' I had tried deflecting his ire onto Vijay by telling him that after all, *I* wasn't the one trying to edge him out, but he still continued to glare at me as if it was all my fault.

We arrived just before lunch at Mum's place and as we sat down, she proudly announced that she'd had Vijay's favourite alu gobi prepared. Now, I had never been a fan of this dish, but after a few months with Vijay I had come to actually abhor it because we had it so often. However, Vijay's eyes lit up at the sight of this preparation and he began to tuck in as if he hadn't eaten in ages.

I had been expecting some delicious non-vegetarian dish, and was vaguely disappointed to note that it was conspicuous by its absence. Further, I strongly suspected that the word had spread about alu gobi being Vijay's favourite food. We were due to visit my grandma and bua over the next two days and I now knew that they too would prepare variations of alu gobi for him and then stand back and watch indulgently as he heaped large portions onto his plate and ate with relish.

I gently suggested to my mother that while this was very nice, hopefully we weren't planning to have alu gobi for each and *every* meal.

My guess about her feeding plan had apparently been fairly accurate and all my tact and sensitivity in the gentle suggestion was rewarded by her snapping back at me, 'Oh, come on. Let him eat. He likes it.'

I decided to persist with, 'Maybe he doesn't like it *all* the time.'

My mother turned her gaze back to Vijay and said in a hurt voice, 'You don't like it, beta?'

'Oh, I like it. I like it,' Vijay immediately assured her through a muffled mouthful, not meeting my gaze.

'Whatever. Alu gobi, alu gobi,' I muttered, adding for good measure, 'everybody loves Vijay.'

My mother ignored me. She fondly watched him eat and murmured, 'Poor Vijay. Probably hardly ever gets to eat this at home. Hain na, beta?'

As Vijay nodded and made a muffled sound in agreement

to this statement, I was rendered speechless. At home, I would typically wave our sporadic part-time cook away uninterestedly every time she asked me what to make – all vegetarian food was the same to me – so she would wander over to Vijay to ask him. He would go into deep thought, looking at the ceiling as if trying to remember some special recipe his grandmother had taught him years ago and eventually say, 'Chalo, alu gobi hi bano do aaj.' Almost every day, it was that damned alu gobi. The one Sunday I had insisted that we have something different, Vijay instructed the cook to try something new.

'So what are we having?' I asked with some interest as it neared lunch time.

'You'll love it, honey. It's a special stuffed paratha …'

I nodded in approval and then asked, 'What's the stuffing?'

The guilty look on his face was more eloquent than words.

I growled at him that I was ordering a pizza and he protested, 'But at least *try* it … have you *ever* had alu gobi paratha?'

And now, even my own family had turned against me, making alu gobi at the drop of a hat. Grossly unfair.

Our time with my mother in Delhi enabled Vijay to get to know her a lot better. On Saturday, I decided that I needed to go to the parlour with my sister, so my mother invited Vijay to go to the Gymkhana Club with her for a beer. As I watched him get ready to accompany her, I remarked sardonically, 'Did you ever think you would be drinking beer with your mother-in-law? So much for all those arranged marriage thingies your parents were setting up for you!'

Vijay looked me up and down in a meaningful way and said, 'Believe me, there is a downside.' He left before I could figure out a good comeback.

I was later told that my mother and Vijay had a pleasant afternoon at the club, talking about different topics but invariably coming back to complaining about how difficult a person I was to live with. At one point during this stimulating exchange, there was a lull and an old tune started playing in the background, one of those tinny piano numbers that are nowadays usually – and rightfully – relegated for use in the elevators of the more old-fashioned hotels. Vijay, always prone to bursting into song after a drink or two, started singing softly, 'De de de de de de re saiba … pyaar mein sauda nahin …'

My mother interrupted him to say, 'It's actually ghe ghe ghe ghe and not de de de de …'

Vijay had to respectfully disagree. '"Ghe ghe"? I don't think so, Mummy – "ghe" is not even a word!'

My mother glared at him. 'As if "de" is a word!'

Vijay realized that this was possibly one of the reasons why my Hindi-speaking skills were not top-notch. 'But Mummy, "de" means "give" in Hindi.'

Mum recovered to continue, 'That's not what I meant. Ghe is Konkani or something. I am not sure, but it's definitely ghe ghe and not de de.' To prove her point, she started singing along to the music. Vijay listened politely and when she had finished the entire song, said mildly, 'Well, that's not how I remember the song, Mummy. But it doesn't matter, does it?' and he deftly changed the subject, probably to some more bitching, with me as the convenient scapegoat.

They finished lunch and came home. After Vijay had his afternoon siesta, he stretched and went out towards the kitchen in the hope that someone would make him a nice refreshing cup of tea.

My mother had apparently been lying in wait for him. She suddenly materialized in the hallway, her laptop balanced on one arm and pounced on him. 'See, Vijay! I googled it … It's ghe ghe and not de de.'

Vijay reeled backwards – never at his best when just awakened from a long nap – and she proceeded to show him how her finding was corroborated by the Youtube video of the song. Frankly, as he later confided in me, it was quite traumatic and not at all in the spirit of the weekend to find your mother-in-law springing at you from dark corners, brandishing heavy objects and shouting incoherent things such as ghe-ghe-de-de in your ear.

It was thus that Vijay discovered that my mother could never lose an argument. Period.

My mother had always been the same. In my childhood, it had been a series of 'I told you so's' and 'Because I said so's' – the former said triumphantly and the latter said in a dangerous tone that you did not argue any further with. But with the advent of technology and the democratization of information, it had become, 'I googled it and here it is! Hah! I told you so.'

More of Mother Dear's quirks were exposed to my husband on this selfsame visit. She had lost her cellphone and wanted to get a new SIM card activated, so she called the nice people at Vodafone for the same. Towards the end of the conversation, the chappy at the other end of the line gave her a fairly long drawn out and extended parting, including wishes for the Guru Purab festival, which happened to be that day.

Hanging up a tad impatiently, my mother tossed the phone on the bed and declared to us, 'These people at Vodafone just memorize dialogues and spew them at the customers mindlessly. He was going on and on … "Chitraji, Chitraji …"' She then proceeded to mimic the man in a breathless, high-pitched tone. 'Chitraji, aapko-aur-aapke-parivaar-ko-Vodafone-ki-tarf-se-iss-Guru-Purab-ke-liye-bahut-bahut-shubhkamnaaye-aapko-Vodafone-call-karne-ki-liye-bahut-bahut-dhanyawaad …'

We laughed at her imitation, but when there was a lull in the merriment, we all became aware of another sound – a tinny voice emanating from her phone, which she had apparently omitted to switch off successfully. 'Chitraji …? Chitraji?' The hapless customer service executive's voice rang quizzically through the room as he attempted to get my mother back on the line.

We all stared at the phone, frozen. Then, mortified, my mother sprang into action, quickly picked up her phone and switched it off, supremely embarrassed. For some reason, she refused to share in our mirth at the situation. And for some reason, her SIM card activation took many days longer than expected.

Later that evening, we were all watching TV together in my mother's room. She wanted to change the channel but was unable to find the remote. She cursed the cleaning lady Parvati for having misplaced it and flitted about the room in a highly irritated frame of mind. She was talking to herself and saying, 'Just look at this woman Parvati, where on earth has she kept the remote control. Of course, she has kept it here behind this chair, in a place where I will never find it.' She looked behind the chair and was surprised to see it wasn't there. 'Oh! Not here? Well, if she had kept it here, I would have found it.' She grumbled to herself some more before remembering something and saying brightly, 'Oh, yes, actually, I think I took it outside when I went to answer the phone and left it there on top of the computer.' She then blissfully trotted off to retrieve it from the other room.

I watched her leave the room in amusement, thinking, 'How weird Mum can be sometimes.' I noticed Vijay giving me a sidelong glance.

'What is it?' I asked.

He checked to make sure my mother was still out of earshot, reached out and held my hand fondly and whispered, 'Honey ... you know ... I finally understand. It's not your fault. I see now where you get it from.'

15

A Home of Our Own

'It's just perfect! I can't believe how perfect it is. Is this a dream? Pinch me, please. Ouch, no, don't, it's just a figure of speech ... never mind!'

Despite my bruised arm, I was ecstatic. Vijay and I were actually buying our very own home together.

It was large, even airier and sunnier than the company-owned flat in which we were currently staying. It was perfectly laid out and within a very nice and well-located new complex, so after clarifying the price and reconfirming the number of zeros in the stated amount, Vijay went ahead and arranged the loan and did all the paperwork and soon we found ourselves landlord and landlady of our very own humble castle.

With the overwhelming realization that this was truly *our* place, we proceeded to set it up exactly the way we wanted.

Our bright-blue sofa set was by now worn but even more comfortable and was of course the central piece of furniture. The television was placed squarely and respectfully in front of it. Our daring combination of curtains, this time in orange, blue and white, decorated the windows.

Perhaps the only classy elements of our décor were the paintings, and these were completely fortuitous acquisitions. In earlier years, Vijay had a struggling artist friend who created more paintings than he could house and Vijay had agreed to take them off his hands. When I had first moved in with Vijay, I had seen these stacked together in the storeroom. The theme of the paintings was jazz: and each was of a man playing a particular musical instrument – the bass guitar, the trumpet, the drums and so on. These weren't exactly abstract but you had to focus to make them out because, interestingly, the artist-friend had gone for the effect of vibration and fuzziness in the paintings, to give the impression of the musicians playing in a smoky little club throbbing with music. They were large paintings in shades of brown, black and white – there were six in all and I thought they were the most beautiful things I had ever seen. Now, in our new flat, Vijay and I finally proceeded to put them up all over the place. I stood back in the living room to admire the effect. It was stunning.

The artist-friend had moved to the US many years before and achieved some success and didn't show any signs of wanting his paintings back. Good thing too, because he would have had to fight me for them. It did occur to me once or twice that if I killed him, their value would go up, but I quashed the thought as an extremely unworthy and shameful one. In any case, I didn't plan to ever sell them.

My mother came to town and helped set up the new flat, presenting us with a pretty wooden nameplate which she had got made for us in Delhi. It said 'Sharmas A-24'. We loved it, even though I couldn't stop myself from muttering something about how it should have said Lal-Sharmas. In fact, we would grow to love this nameplate so much that we would later use it for all our subsequent homes, thus turning away many a confused would-be visitor, who would call and say, 'But I was looking for 1-D, and it said A-24.' For the moment, we just thanked my mother warmly and hammered it on the wall outside the apartment in a solemn little ceremony. We stood back to admire the effect. Sharmas, A-24. It looked pretty cool.

One of my favourite spots in our new home was the balcony – it faced the outside of the complex. We liked this fact because it meant that we would get some privacy. The only thing that marred an otherwise perfectly lovely view was a most unsightly yellow building some distance away, which was an eyesore to end all eyesores. Still, if we ignored this building, the landscape around was green and pretty and the mild weather of Bangalore made most mornings there an absolute pleasure. Vijay and I had many heart-to-heart, if slightly one-sided, conversations over steaming cups of tea, made, of course, by my own expert hands.

The new flat was on the second floor in a well-laid-out, green and spacious complex, which had its own swimming pool and club house. We never actually used either of these but it felt good to know they were there. The complex also had its own basketball court and this was something that we actually *did* use a lot. I had played basketball in school and was a pretty sharp shooter. However, Vijay had a good nine-inch height advantage over me and this made it difficult for me to beat him. In all our one-on-ones, he would lope past me like a graceful giraffe and score basket after basket. Since I was not a very good loser, I started resorting to more aggressive defense techniques such as pulling down his track pants just as he was about to shoot – a simple pleasure he took away from me by tying his nadas tighter. But we still played almost every day after work.

Unlike most other new constructions in Bangalore, our complex consisted of many buildings spread over a large area of land, each building only four floors high. This was a blessing and one of the primary reasons we had chosen to live here – because it meant that we were not living in large concrete towers, but within fairly small attractively-designed buildings. This also meant a lot of terraces though, for some reason, Vijay and I were the only people who actually chose to use these terraces. In fact, on nights when the weather was particularly pleasant, we dragged heavy razais onto the terrace of our building and fell asleep there, under the bright moon, watching the luminous clouds as they drifted past. On clear nights, we looked up at the stars.

It was on one such beautiful, slightly chilly night, as we lay together under the stars, that I found myself filled with a sense of complete bliss.

Suddenly, Vijay said, 'Look – a shooting star!'

'Quick,' I cried. 'Make a wish!'

'Oh … okay! … I wish …'

'To yourself,' I hissed, fervently making my own wish, eyes shut tight.

It came to me very simply. I wished with all my might that we would find great happiness in this, our very own

home, till the end of our days – or at least for many more
years to come.

16

Bye Bye Bangalore

'What do you *mean*, moving to Mumbai?' I cried.

It had barely been a month since we had set up our
own home and now Vijay was suggesting that we leave
Bangalore?

He seemed to realize that casually springing this on me
over breakfast hadn't been the best idea. He asked me to calm
down, gently taking away the quivering butter knife that I
had been unconsciously brandishing.

'I meant to tell you last night but then I forgot … There's
an open position for business head for Rural in the Mumbai
office … it's my chance to get out of marketing, so I was
thinking I'd apply for it … Madhukar said I've got a good
chance of getting it …' His voice trailed off.

I seethed. Vijay had a habit of forgetting to tell me the
most important things, but this was the limit. The previous
night, he had bored me stiff with a detailed description of
his conversation about cricket with the tea-boy Jaggan, but
had omitted to tell me about a career move he was discussing
with his boss?

This role apparently involved heading a relatively new
and progressive initiative of the company, a project which
distributed its products to the smallest villages in the country,
while providing a living to the distributors of these products
– usually underprivileged women. Vijay was very taken with

this concept because he had, for a long time, dreamt of doing 'something meaningful'. I had to admit that the role did sound like the very thing for him and muttered my unwilling agreement that he should give it a shot, in any case.

But why did it have to be based in bloody Mumbai?

I had a bad feeling that Vijay would end up getting the new job. He had always been very different from the regular hard-core-corporate-types and had a passion for do-gooding that somehow struck me as highly suitable for a slightly off-the-beaten-track initiative such as the rural project.

But every fibre of my being was resistant to the idea of leaving Bangalore. I sat alone moodily on the chair in the balcony that evening, looking out at the view I loved – including even that unsightly yellow eyesore of a building that I decided had actually been growing on me of late. I didn't want to move to unknown bustling Mumbai.

I reflected upon how Bangalore had been a great place to be a young, slightly asinine couple getting to know each other. Although we had plenty of impetuous weekend trips out of the city, we had also, over the last year, enjoyed pottering about the various parks, pubs, malls and busy streets of Bangalore. On the rare occasions that we were not slaving away at our desks, we could be found eating bhutta, chaat, and other street food, idly exploring second-hand bookstores – or watching the Govinda movies that Vijay would drag me to kicking and screaming.

It was during one of these idle explorations of the city streets that we had bought ourselves bicycles. For most people, a purchase of this nature is not what we marketeers term an 'impulse purchase'. Those are usually things like a bag of chips or maybe a chocolate. But in our case, one minute, we were just walking around MG Road, holding hands and gnawing on our bhuttas and the next minute, we were struggling to fit two brand-new, gleaming bicycles – his dark blue, mine a pretty purple – into the trunk of our car. We had decided on the spur of the moment that this would be a good investment as it would give us some much needed exercise and also enable us to explore the surrounding landscape, since there were some undeveloped green areas and even a forgotten lake near our new home. It had led to a total of about seven pleasant cycling excursions for us, and personally, about two near-death experiences for me.

Shortly after this new purchase, Vijay received a cryptic text message from an unfamiliar number on his phone which, for one shocked and awed moment, we assumed to be a message from God – or maybe an eerily accurate horoscope-on-SMS service. It said 'Yashodhara should not ride a cycle in heavy traffic areas.' We were hugely impressed by this until further investigation revealed it to be Papaji's first ever attempt at text messaging on the new cellphone that Vijay had imposed upon him recently. It turned out that Mummyji had heard about our cycling excursions and taken it upon herself to worry about it and had urged Papaji to intervene.

She needn't have worried. Shortly after this, both our bicycles were stolen by some unscrupulous visitors to our apartment complex. That night, as on every other night, we had trotted off home and left them parked outside, unlocked – with our trademark innocent trust in the world that some people, especially my mother, called carelessness. So that was the end of that.

It was the other little things too that made me attached to Bangalore. It was an eminently musical city – approximately every third person here appeared to be able to play a musical instrument. In fact, I thought sadly, what would become of my drum lessons?

I had recently started these under the tutelage of a young man with the extremely engaging name of Ryan Mario Crispin Colaco. He was the drummer for a band called Kryptos and had what Vijay termed 'bhayanak talent'.

I would later come to know the kind of fan following Ryan had amongst music lovers but at that point, he was somebody whose number I had got from someone else. When I spoke to him on the phone to set up my first lesson, we planned to meet outside the Lifestyle mall near his house. I waited a tad nervously for him to show up. Suddenly, a really tall, dark, well-built man sporting a French beard with his long hair in a ponytail came walking up to me. He matched the mental picture that I had formed of Ryan and I became even more nervous. Just as I was reaching out to shake his hand, he walked past me and as I looked after him in confusion, a voice behind me rang out, 'Yashodhara?'

I turned to see a skinny, fair young man who was nearly a head shorter than me. This was the real Ryan Mario Crispin Colaco. His languid gait, extremely long curly hair and the fact that the smell of smoke lingered about him identified him as a real Rocker. We shook hands and I grinned at him as he led me to his house to start up the lessons. This dude wasn't scary at all.

Ryan was humorous, talented and would turn out to be a great teacher. It was another matter that I didn't practise at home at all and therefore never made any real progress, though he assured me that I 'had the rhythm within me'. Clearly, it wasn't going to come out anytime soon, but I had fun during the weekend lessons anyway – although I got a bigger kick out of just hearing him play new and incredibly complicated beats.

The booming of the drums rang out all over his old-fashioned two-storied independent house. Ryan's rather elderly parents were very nice, although I got the impression from their wan smiles that they still wished their young rocker son would get a 'real job'. However, their resigned air implied that they had given up on this hope a long time ago.

And now, I would have to give up on their son because I was leaving the city I loved.

Over the next few days, as Vijay was confirmed as the preferred candidate for the rural head position, I eventually reconciled myself to the idea of the move; one had to support one's spouse in the pursuit of their dream. In any case, at work, it was time for me to move on, and frankly, loyal brand manager to my wonderful tea brand though I was, there was only so much time you could spend peddling boring tea without getting completely fed up of it. While I would have preferred to stay in Bangalore, I decided that Mumbai it would be. Enjoying the unfamiliar feeling of martyrdom, I decided to go shopping for a surprise present for Vijay. I would use it to congratulate him for the new post and to communicate to him that I was okay with the move.

I had racked my brains and thought of the perfect surprise present for him. He had told me that one of his fondest memories of his childhood in Jaipur was that of his father setting up a telescope on the terrace of their house for many happy nights of star-gazing. I figured that now that he would be visiting small villages where the night sky would be clear, a telescope would be just the thing for him.

He was touched when I presented him with a wrapped box, saying, 'You shouldn't have, honey. What is it?'

'Open it and see.' I was eager to see his reaction.

He unwrapped the box and lifted the lid to find a foot-long, sleek, black, impressive looking telescope. He lifted it and fingered it wonderingly. 'Wow! This is so cool. But why?'

I waited a while for him to continue, until I realized that he was not referring to me by the convenient nickname he had devised for me by simply shortening my name to the first alphabet. I explained my logic and solemnly wished him many pleasant nights of reviving his old astronomical hobby by star-gazing from the villages.

He touched my face and said, 'This is the sweetest thing you've ever done for me. It's really thoughtful.'

As I glowed with happiness, he examined the box and saw the price tag which I had forgotten to remove.

He was quiet for a moment and then said, 'Y. Is this correct? Fifteen *thousand* rupees?'

I nodded. I had figured a high-end version made sense if you were serious about a hobby. The stars were rather far away, after all. Only the best for my Vijay.

The next day, I sulked for most of the day on the balcony, as he went back to the mall and exchanged the telescope for a new digital camera.

And a short two months later, we had wrapped up our life in Bangalore and had moved to the mad city of Mumbai.

PART II

I Get By With a Little Help from My Help

'What a view, eh, hon? Look at the waves ... Look at that boat ... hey, look, is that couple actually making out? Hawww ... where's our video camera? I love Bandstand!'

We had moved from languid, pleasant Bangalore to Mumbai, the city where I immediately and penetratingly observed that people walked much too fast. With some luck, persistence and by making the lives of a couple of admin people a living hell, we had successfully wangled a company apartment on Bandstand with the most amazing sea view imaginable.

We had already started work at our new jobs in Mumbai – Vijay in his new rural business head role and I as brand manager for a shampoo brand. Dandruff removal seemed so much sexier than trying to convince people that tea was healthy. Except it really wasn't and I found that I was now merely one of approximately a hundred managers for this international brand, with many teams involved at the local, regional and global level. In fact, it was my private suspicion that there were some teams at the interplanetary level, too, but these forces remained unseen. In short, I wasn't enjoying this job as much as the previous one.

Our new place was a relief, though. It was really tiny, a basic two-bedroom apartment barely half the size of our Bangalore home – but big enough for the two of us, as long as we didn't move around too much. It was on the third floor of the building, very close to Shah Rukh Khan's bungalow; we had already started letting it slip into casual conversation that we were now 'Shah Rukh's neighbours'. Our apartment had huge windows in the bedroom and living room, overlooking the sea. These windows had earlier been barred with ugly grills as part of the 'company standard safety policy', which said that unbarred windows were unsafe for small children. But we had got them removed using the strong argument that we had no children and didn't plan on ever having any, small or otherwise. The removal of the grills had a spectacular effect on the place and with the windows now opening out onto the big blue sea, the flat cleverly gave the impression of being twice as large as it really was.

Vijay finally stopped pointing out the couples who were making out in public and we fell silent as the sun slowly started to set over the sea, making for a lovely scene in hues of orange and grey. We stood there, side by side, holding hands – a young husband and wife basking in the quiet contentment of being together, enjoying a brief respite between harried moments of unpacking.

And then the silence was shattered by a blaring high-pitched voice ringing through the apartment.

'MAIN TUMHARE LIYE CHAI BANATEEE?'

Startled, we turned towards the door from which the voice had emanated. A short, sari-clad wizened old woman stood gazing enquiringly at us through thick spectacles.

Vijay took charge of the situation and said, 'Chai? Haan, haan, chai. Par ... aap ho kaun?'

The old woman suddenly seemed to remember her manners and showed all her surprisingly white teeth in what was probably meant to be an ingratiating grin. 'MAIN

ZARREENA. ISS BUILDING MEIN MAIN-ICH KAAM KARTEEE. SAB FLOOR PE MAIN-ICH. EK FLOOR, DO FLOOR, CHAAR FLOOR, SAB FLOOR.' She added in a revealing tone, 'TUM TEEN FLOOR PE HO.'

While we were still developing our response to this indisputable statement, Zarreena went ahead and rummaged around in our new kitchen and informed us loudly that we didn't have any tea powder. Undaunted, she went over to one of the many other flats in the building which she apparently ruled and used the raw materials and utensils there to prepare and bring down two steaming cups of tea for us. I was immediately impressed by her resourcefulness and decided she was exactly what we needed. While sipping the tea, I quietly but firmly impressed upon Vijay that we should hire her and he shouldn't try his negotiation tricks on her and drive her away. This tended to happen when he bargained with people, since his idea of negotiation was to bid one-twentieth of the initial price. He reluctantly agreed.

After the brief debate on her salary which she won, she demanded of Vijay, 'MERA CHAABEE KAHAN HAIN?'

Vijay was taken aback and clearly uncomfortable with trusting a complete stranger with the house key, so he said, 'Chaabee nahin dega.'

Zarreena looked both shocked and hurt. 'KYOON?'

Vijay couldn't bring himself to say that he didn't trust her yet, so came up with an inspired 'Uhh … ek hi hain!'

Zarreena guffawed at this tiny problem and said, 'MERE KO DEYO. MAIN BANWA KE AATEE, NAA. PHATAFAT BANWA KE AATEE.'

Defeated, Vijay mutely handed over the key. She disappeared and was back soon, with two extra copies of the key which she gave to us. And then she proceeded to take over the house.

Over the next few days, as we continued to settle ourselves into our new jobs, we were delighted to discover that we could leave most things regarding the house to Zarreena – she would not only cook for us, including early morning tea, breakfast and dinner, but also take care of the other household chores like cleaning, buying veggies, getting the clothes ironed and so on. It was great – like having a live-in maid without her actually living in.

Zarreena had her little drawbacks, of course – the chief of which was her disinclination to fold clothes and put them into cupboards. She preferred to put them straight into the washing machine, regardless of whether they actually needed cleaning or not. I would buy many new clothes, try them on once and leave them around, only to find them hanging out to dry the next day. And since she would enthusiastically and indiscriminately bung everything into what was clearly her favourite invention in the world, more than one wonderfully expensive new shirt was tainted with the bright colour of a cheap undie – Vijay's, of course.

The other drawback was that once she got into a chatty mood, it was difficult to end the conversation. She would address me out of the blue, interrupting my reading with a conversational, 'MADAM, MAIN SAARA HINDUSTAN KE LIYE KAAM KIYA.'

I would be genuinely impressed by this. 'Achha? Saara desh mein?'

Zarreena would clarify, 'NAHINNN! TUMHARA COMPANY KA SAARA LOG YAHAN REHTA NA. KITNA SAHIB AAYA-GAYA – SAB KE LIYE MAIN-ICH KAAM KIYA.'

'Oh, achha. Hindustan Products Limited ke log ki liye.'

Zarreena was not one to bother with the details. 'HAAN –
WO-ICH TOH MAIN BHI BOLI – SAARA HINDUSTAN
– TUMHARE PEHLA KAUNSA MADRASI YAHAN
THA? MOTA SAHIB?'

I, of course, had no clue as to the real identity of the
gentleman she referred to as Mota Sahib, but she insisted
that I hazard a guess. And this would cue the beginning of
the never-ending game of us trying to establish who lived in
the apartment before Vijay and me and who before them,
and so on, ending only when it was sundown and time for
her to go home.

Vijay and I had decided that the distances and traffic
situation in Mumbai warranted the hiring of a driver – it
was not a luxury but a necessity, we told ourselves. However,
hiring the driver proved to be easier said than done.

For one, Vijay insisted on very exacting standards when
it came to our driver and grilled the aspiring applicants quite
heavily on their backgrounds, their knowledge of driving and
so on before rejecting most on grounds like 'He looked at
me a bit funnily.' For another, he wasn't prepared to pay the
going rate and his usual over-baked attempts at bargaining –
including feigning a heart attack at what they quoted – drove
away a good many prospects.

Desperate to avoid the three hours of driving to and from
work, Vijay decided to start taking new prospective drivers
to office and back 'on trial'. After a day or two of this, they
would apparently decide that he didn't quite cut it as a
potential employer and disappeared, melting away into the
crowds of Mumbai, without even asking for any payment.
Vijay claimed that this suited him just fine because it meant

free rides to work, but I said that it was probably his incessant backseat driving that put them off, and told him that at this rate we would never find a reliable driver.

And then, along came Vinod.

Vinod was a young driver who was introduced to us by one of the security guards of our building. I liked him immediately because he was well-turned-out, bright-eyed and alert. He was slightly built and his eyes were a unique greyish-green colour. He seemed much younger than his stated age of twenty-three and he cultivated a thin moustache possibly to try and look older.

Vijay took him for the 'trial period' and was quite satisfied with his driving skills, which he had apparently perfected at the age of seven while learning to drive his father's tractor up a few hills in his village near Allahabad in Uttar Pradesh. Without too much negotiation on the salary for once, Vinod was hired.

Over the next few days, I discovered I liked having a driver, particularly this one. When I approached the car, he would appear out of nowhere like a shot to open the door for me, greyish-green eyes twinkling as he politely wished me good morning. He always helped with the shopping bags and would run after me to give me my cellphone, purse or whatever item I had left behind in the car. He never missed a day of work, always arrived half an hour early and never complained about being called too early or being kept too late – in fact, often, he would even land up on his day off – Sunday – of his own accord, just to see if he could drive us somewhere. Soon, he started doing our grocery shopping for us as well.

Vinod also politely put up with Vijay's backseat driving and contrary instructions like 'Koi jaldi nahin … aaram se chalaao …' followed by 'Late ho rahen hain … thoda daudao.' He didn't needlessly chat while driving, but when he did speak, it was amusing to hear his overly polite, sing-song lilt saying in response to our probing 'Hume gaon nahin jaana, wahan bore hote hain … hamare papa-mummy kehte hain shaadi kar lo, par hume shaadi nahin karni …'

It turned out that Vinod had previously worked for one 'Model Memsahib', some sort of upcoming starlet who was very fussy and difficult and used to keep him out driving all day and all night. This was possibly one reason why he appeared to consider Vijay and me employers of the century – the benchmark was very low.

But thanks to having worked for Model Memsahib, Vinod knew the party places in Mumbai better than we did. If we ever asked, 'Vinod, Hawaiian Shack maalum hain?' he would shoot back a quick 'Ji, sir' with quiet confidence and take off without further ado.

He had also been exposed to the stars and drivers of the stars due to the socializing activities of his Model Memsahib. He told us, 'Jab Model Memsahib hume Sanjay Dutt ke ghar le gayi toh unhone hume dekh ke poocha, "Tu baarah saal ka hain, kya?" Aur phir hume paanch hazaar rupaiye diye.' Here he paused respectfully, a hint of nostalgia and gratitude in his eyes. He then added, 'Bahut peete hain.'

The arrogance of certain members of tinsel town had earned Vinod's disapproval. 'Shah Rukh Khan ka driver kissi se baat nahin karta … sochta hain, "Main Shah Rukh Khan ka driver hoon".'

Another time, he confided in me, 'Arjun Rampal apne aap ko issuper-ishtar samajhta hain – par uss ke paas toh sirf ek Ford Endeavour hain.' The biting scorn with which he made the last announcement made it clear what he thought of Arjun Rampal and his claim to stardom.

Vinod, of course, had his faults as well. He had a temper which he rarely displayed in front of me, but was apparently always willing to pick a fight if he deemed another to be driving badly. He had a lot of self-confidence – misplaced, in my belief – in his ability to beat up anyone if necessary. 'Hum mein bahut taakat hain, madam,' he said to me once and I nodded while casting a doubtful eye over his skinny frame, estimating him to weigh about ten kilos less than me.

Vinod also tended to drive faster than necessary and sometimes had to be chastised by Vijay for this. I never noticed, as I was usually gazing dreamily out of the window at nothing and in any case, he seemed to be a bit protective of me because he once confided to a colleague of mine, 'Jab madam hoti hain gaadi mein, toh main hamesha araam se chalaata hoon.'

One evening, about a month after joining us, he admitted to having been in a scrap with the law and we were very interested in knowing the details.

He said, 'Sir, aaj hamara license chala gaya. Kal court se collect karna hain.'

'Kyon, kya hua?'

Vinod explained, 'Ek police-waala aaya aur hum sab driver pe chillaane laga ... bola ki humne wrong parking ki hui hain. Par humne nahin ki thi, sir. Uss ke saath sab driver log ladne lage ... aur ... aur hume bhi gussa aa gaya, sir! Humne bhi police-waale ko keh diya!'

Vijay really wanted to know where this would go. 'Toh kya kaha tumne?'

Vinod seemed too ashamed to continue. 'Poochiye mat, sir ... bas keh diya.'

Vijay coaxed him, getting ready to hear the choicest of Allahabadi abuses, 'Bolo, na ... kya kahaan ... gaali de di kya?'

Vinod said with the air of someone getting something heavy off his chest, 'Sir … humne police waale ko poochha, "Tumhe hawaldar *banaya* kisne?"'

And that was Vinod.

So there was no denying that we now had good help. Also indisputable was the beautiful sea view. But still, I missed our own home in Bangalore and the city itself. I found myself resenting Vijay's insistence on moving to Mumbai due to some mad, completely inexplicable urge to experience sales in rural India. I tried to adjust to the situation and not complain, given that it had only been a short while since our move. Besides, at least *he* seemed to be enjoying his new job a lot more than the previous one, even though it was the opposite for me. But after all, sacrifice was what marriage was all about, right?

It sucked.

2

The Social Circle

'I really think we need to be more social,' I announced to Vijay one evening as we sat alone in our sea-facing apartment.

It had been on my mind of late that despite our many similarities to Monica and Chandler, one thing that was strikingly different was that we had no friends to have coffee and laugh with on a daily basis. I was already beginning to visualize us in later years and wondered – when he and I turned eighty and seventy-three respectively, would we be the sort of antisocial, doddering old couple who would have no one to share their park bench with? Or more possibly,

I thought, we might not even live to such an age since, according to some research report I had read on the internet, the higher rate of longevity was observed amongst people who maintained close relationships with friends throughout their lives.

The fact was that Vijay and I had been so wrapped up in each other for the last year or so that we didn't hang out regularly with anyone else. I was still shuddering at the thought of imminent death by lack of bosom buddies, when Vijay agreed with me readily about our need to socialize.

'Sure,' he said and added after a pause, 'but with whom?'

I thought about it for a while and then admitted defeat. There was absolutely no one to socialize with. The problem was that while we were intermittently in touch with our older friends, Vijay and I still hadn't found anyone we could *both* hang out with.

Vijay had once attributed this to the fact that I didn't like any of his friends' wives.

'But they don't like me,' I protested.

Vijay raised an eyebrow and I admitted, 'Oh, all right – it's just that they are boring aunty-types.'

Since Vijay was so much older than me, so were his friends and their wives. They were all slightly balding, slightly potbellied and had moustaches – the husbands that is, at least mostly – and of course, they also had their precious children whom they were always going on and on about.

I decided to go on the offensive. 'You don't like any of *my* friends either.'

'That's because they are all immature brats, just like y–' Vijay saw the look in my eye in the nick of time, checked himself and pretended to have a coughing fit.

In Bangalore too, it had only been towards the last few

months that we had discovered that one of my friends, Manav, actually met with Vijay's approval.

'Yeah, he's one decent guy – can't think of anything wrong with him,' Vijay had admitted, a trifle reluctantly.

After this, we had insisted that poor Manav spend all his free time with us, telling him that he was 'our social circle'. Evening after evening, he would find himself sitting on our sofa while we chastized him for spending too much time at work and told him that he really should make more time for us.

Since Vijay and I had started hanging around with him so often, Manav was an unwilling witness to many of our arguments. He would find himself sitting around and twiddling his thumbs nervously while Vijay and I glared at each other in stony silence. He would eventually say, 'Chalo, main nikalta hoon,' and make as if to get up, but we would both turn towards him quickly and I would bark, 'Sit, Manav. You are our social circle. You keep us sane.' Vijay would nod along sullenly in agreement while Manav would sink back gloomily into his chair. And Vijay and I would go back to glaring stonily at each other while Manav recommenced twiddling his thumbs.

When we were leaving Bangalore, Manav seemed really eager to aid the process – he insisted on coming over to help us pack. He lifted heavy boxes with an unusual degree of enthusiasm and even drove us to the airport for our flight to Mumbai. I thought I saw tears in his eyes when it was time to say goodbye – possibly tears of joy.

Now that we were starting afresh in Mumbai, I was determined that the two of us would have a social life. After a great deal of reflection, I finally realized the problem.

'You know what?' I said brightly to Vijay. 'The issue is that we don't have even one solid, good set of *couple*-friends. Couple-friends are very important. Then we can do all sorts of couple-things together … like … like …'

'Tennis doubles?' Vijay suggested helpfully.

'… trips and stuff,' I finished a trifle lamely, distracted by his interference.

'Sounds like a good idea,' he said. 'Got anyone in mind?'

I thought about it. 'Well, almost all my batchmates are here – Atul is newly married …'

'No way,' he interjected. 'No newly married couples. They are always all kootchy-kooey and annoying to be around.'

'You mean like we were back in our younger days, when we were actually romantic with each other?'

'Exactly,' he shuddered. 'Awful.'

'Okayyy then,' I said. 'Should we go with your friends? Who do you know here?'

Vijay frowned and said, 'Hmmm. There is this guy I knew at IIT, Mohit – he's quite cool … I've met his wife also … Sheila or something …'

'They got kids?'

'Yes, two …'

'Next!' I said firmly.

'Listen, Y,' Vijay said earnestly. 'This way we'll never find anyone to hang out with together. You know what I think? Let's just go with the flow and see what happens, right? Go about our lives as usual and strike up new friendships in a natural way. It has to be spontaneous.'

'Fine, fine.' I agreed, but then a thought struck me and I continued, 'Or, we could look at someone from our office. That way, we'll all have something in common …'

'Yes, that sounds spontaneous,' agreed Vijay, his voice

dripping with sarcasm. 'Why don't you put up a sign on the noticeboard? I can see it now ... "Wanted. Office Couple for Friendship with Like Minded Twosome. Acceptable Age Range Thirty-two to Thirty-four Only. Should Have No Issues. Must Live Near Bandstand. Female Half Should Ideally Be Hot Stuff" ... Wait, wait, honey! Come back ... help me craft the job description ... ha ha ha ha ...'

As it turned out, our eventual couple-friends did indeed turn out to be someone from our office – at least one of them was.

Vivita, ubiquitously known as Vivi, worked on the same shampoo brand that I did and I had been warned about her by my colleagues: 'Watch out for her – she's really weird.' I was usually undaunted by weirdness. But once I met Vivi, I could see the point.

Vivi was the type of person who had no compunction with occasionally coming to office in the clothes in which she had slept the previous night. She had a flat on the office campus and reported to somebody in the regional team in Bangkok and being fond of her beauty sleep, she did not enjoy the early morning telephone conversations 'with Bangkok' as she put it, which were typically scheduled at 8 a.m. Therefore, on those days, she preferred to dispense with the formality of dressing and appeared wearing brightly coloured slippers and pyjamas, her short hair dishevelled, participating intermittently in the conversation with Bangkok on the speakerphone.

She confided to me that she had once participated in a telecon from her bathroom at home and no one had figured it out. 'It was very early in the morning and I can't just *go* like that, you know? I need my time on the pot.' I thought this fell in the category of 'too much information', but nodded along.

Apart from the sloppiness of the aforementioned early mornings, Vivi was a sharp dresser. She even had a range of stylish saris which she wore for important meetings and her unique fashion sense made her stand out in the corporate environment.

She walked into the office one day, tall in her fashionably high heels, resplendent in a dark blue shimmery sari, her short hair all shiny and neatly styled with some sort of gel or spray. While we were exchanging pleasantries, I thought to myself that she looked wonderfully elegant today. Exactly at this point, she suddenly paused, ran her tongue over her teeth and declared, 'Oh, you know what? I think I forgot to brush today!' She then trotted over to the oral care department to borrow a sample pack of toothpaste and a spare toothbrush and headed to a nearby loo to correct her oversight.

Another time, all the managers in our company were to attend a speech given by an important British vice-president from the global headquarters. About half an hour into his speech, the door at the front of the auditorium, right next to the stage, creaked open and Madame Vivi poked her head through it. Undaunted by the fact that all eyes were staring at her, she boldly entered. After a couple of seconds, she seemed to lose her nerve slightly, but it was too late to turn back. So she scanned the packed room and spotted one empty seat right at the back and started heading for it. Unfortunately her attempt at subtly tiptoeing to it was rendered somewhat ineffective by the fact that she was wearing her most stylish heels that day. The bemused speaker's speech was now punctuated by her quick 'tick-tock-tick-tock's. She soon realized that she was being a disruptive influence and slowed down and began to take really long, slow strides in a manner reminiscent of the Pink Panther. All this did was to lengthen the space between each tick-tock, so it became 'tick ... tock ... tick ... tock' instead. The speaker cleared his throat a couple of times, but being of the foreign variety, politely continued talking and made no allusion to her, in spite of the fact that he had now lost the attention of almost everyone in the audience.

Vivi finally settled into her seat and having regained her innate self-confidence, began looking around her and scanning the faces of all the people staring at her. She spotted me a few seats away and flashed me a friendly grin and waved excitedly. I resisted my first impulse to pretend that I didn't know her and after a second, smiled and nodded back at her.

'This,' I thought Casablanca-style, 'could be the beginning of a beautiful friendship.'

Vivi and her bespectacled, lanky husband Anshul came over for dinner one evening and despite Vijay's scepticism, which stemmed from my various confused attempts over the last few days to describe Vivi as a person, we all got along well. We sat in our living room, windows thrown open, the sound and smell of the waves outside creating just the right atmosphere for us to get to know each other. Vivi had a laugh that was penetrating and infectious, like a bell which clanged around inside your head, in a nice way, of course. She spotted my guitar lying around and demanded that I play it – I complied and as I strummed, she sang along in a loud, clear, confident and almost completely tuneless voice.

It was revealed that Vivi had an unshakeable and possibly rather misplaced belief in her own talents. Some years back, she confided, she had seen an ad in the paper calling for singers and actors for a part in a musical being staged by a theatre group that travelled the world for their performances. Vivi called up her mother to prepare her for the fact that her daughter would shortly be quitting her corporate job and travelling the world, performing. Her mother, who appeared to have the same blind faith in her talents, assured her that she would be supporting her completely in this life-altering decision. Vivi went ahead for the audition, preparing the song 'Somewhere Over the Rainbow'. She performed confidently – and after only a few moments of stunned silence, the judges politely informed her that they were looking for an alto while she was clearly a soprano. Listening to her sing now, I could fully sympathize with them.

As the evening progressed, I noticed that Vijay seemed to be taking a shine to the earnest and slightly geeky Anshul, and was talking to him in a fairly animated way. Vivi and I were discussing movies and for a moment, the men paused to listen to our conversation.

'Have you seen this movie, *French Kiss*? It's quite sweet.'

'I've seen it and thought it was rather silly,' was Vivi's response.

'It is silly of course, but it's also rather funny. Meg Ryan is cute in it and I even liked Kevin Kline's role.'

At this, Anshul turned to Vijay and asked in a low voice, 'Kevin Kline? Yeh kaun hain?'

Vijay explained confidently, 'Wo chaddi hoti hain na …'

I was aghast. 'No, that's *Calvin* Klein. And is that all you have to say about a brand like that? *Chaddi?*'

Anshul rushed to Vijay's defense. 'Arrey, nahin, yaar, *achhi* chaddi hoti hain …'

It looked like Vijay and I had found our couple-friends.

As the evening drew to a close, I sighed with satisfaction. Now that we had our social circle in place, we were finally all set to enjoy Mumbai – and the carefree, fun days ahead.

3

I'm WHAT?

I stood there in the cubicle of the toilet in our Churchgate office, staring at the little white strip with two pink lines on it. A range of emotions passed over me in a dizzying wave.

Shock. We were using protection. How could this be? We were just not ready for it.

Anger. This was all Vijay's fault. Obviously. Everything was always his fault – but this time, it really was.

Suspicion. Could he have tampered with the protection? He had been going on about wanting a kid 'someday soon' since our wedding night.

Resentment. I was still only in my twenties, it was my time for self-exploration. What would happen to those various thrilling adventures that had yet to show up? What about my plans of climbing Mt Kilimanjaro? Okay, I hadn't actually had any such plans, but now, I *couldn't* very well have them, could I?

And then there was the fear. I was clearly going to be a horrible mother. Could you be too sarcastic to be a mother? Was there some sort of threshold limit?

I leaned weakly against the door of the toilet and sighed. The truth of the matter was that I still hadn't experienced any sort of maternal pangs. I continued to be firm in my belief that children were pests who should be neither seen nor heard. They were too short, you couldn't ever hope to have an adult conversation with one and in general, in my closely guarded and privately held opinion, they were best described in the simple phrase 'slightly icky'.

Except that this one was going be *my* icky child. Correction – *our* icky child.

Still in a daze, I slipped the pregnancy test into my purse – perhaps not the most hygienic move to make. I stepped out of the toilet and went to the third floor of the office, where I knew Vijay would be. We generally didn't have much time for conversation while at the office, but in my judgement, this recent discovery fell in the category of those terribly serious conversations between married couples that begin with 'we need to talk.'

He was sitting at his desk and as I came up silently behind him, I saw that he was busy working at his laptop on some fancy excel file with sales numbers on it. I leaned over and said in a low, serious voice, 'We need to talk.'

Without looking up, he said, 'We-need-to-talk toh theek hain, par yeh kya number diye hain, saale?' He was pointing to a row in the excel file. I stayed silent until he looked up at me. 'Oh, hi. It's you? I thought it was Satyendu. Why are you talking like a man?'

I bristled at being mistaken for his male team member. Wordlessly, I snapped open my purse to show him the ultimate proof of my femininity, if ever there was one.

He looked down and winced. 'No, thanks. How old is that Kit-kat anyway? Do you ever clean this out?'

Irritated, I shoved my hand deeper into the purse, brushing the half-eaten bar of Kitkat and a few colorful rubberbands and pens aside and dug out the pregnancy test. Looking around to see that no one was watching us, I held it up for him to see and hissed, 'No, dummy. I'm pregnant.'

His brown eyes did their familiar shifty, fast-as-lightning flicker all around the room to confirm that no one was eavesdropping. A slow smile spread itself over his face. He whispered, 'You're pregnant? Really? Wow!' And then his Florence Nightingale instincts kicked in and he jumped up to get me a chair. 'You better sit down.'

I plopped into the offered chair and was immediately bombarded with questions. 'Are you sure about this? How do you feel? Have you been throwing up? Would you like something to eat?'

Not knowing which question to answer first, I just looked at him for a minute. Eventually I decided to go in chronological order and said, 'Well, that's what this test says. I'm a bit shocked. I haven't been puking and no, I don't want anything to eat.'

'But you should! You should eat something. You should eat lots! We'll go to some lab right away and reconfirm. We'll …' He then appeared to be assailed by a sudden doubt and said more carefully, 'Honey? We *are* going to have this baby, right?'

I was surprised by this question and also surprised that the thought of *not* having the baby hadn't even occurred to me. But most of all, I was surprised at the conviction in my voice when the words came out of my mouth: 'Of course we are!'

If there had been any doubt in my mind about the decision, it was wiped away by the grin of pure happiness that my husband flashed at me. I recalled the many instances when he had subtly and not-so-subtly conveyed his readiness to be a father. Now he said it slowly, savouring the sound of the words on his tongue, 'A real little baby of our own.'

He squeezed my hand in excitement and as he got a wondering and faraway look in his eyes, I sensed it was a good time to put down a few practical conditions. 'So we'll do it this way. The first nine months are mine, you handle the next nine ...'

We reconfirmed through the laboratory test later in the day that I was indeed pregnant. Over the next few days, I commenced my research and preparation.

I viewed this as my most important personal project to date and was determined to do a thorough job in terms of gathering the requisite information. I eyed with some satisfaction my thick, shiny new copy of the pregnancy bible *What to Expect When You're Expecting*. I had caught Vijay giving it what appeared to be a sceptical look and had immediately pounced on him, informing him that 'If you've got to do something, you better do it right.' He said something about going with the flow, being a natural with kids and relying on the knowledge in the family about this kind of thing. But when I looked at him thoughtfully and suggested that perhaps we should get him his *own* copy to read, he beat a hasty retreat and left me to it.

The internet opened up a whole new world of pregnancy-related information and I signed up on multiple websites to get weekly updates as to how my baby was growing in the womb.

Almost immediately, I found myself developing all sorts of uncomfortable symptoms. The more I read, the more I realized how awful I was feeling. I went through the check-list of the various problems I had.

Nausea: Naturally.

Dizziness: But of course.

Back Pain: Indubitably.

Gum-bleeding: You betcha.

Pre-eclampsia: I wasn't sure what this one was but when I found out, I was going to have it.

But above all, it was the nausea that really took everything I had out of me. Quite literally.

The worst part of the early days of my pregnancy was that I was simply unable to keep any form of food down. Everything tasted awful, whether on the way down or on the way up. This, combined with the kind of exhaustion that I had never known before, made me crabbier than I had ever been. And this was probably saying something.

Vijay was bearing it all with great fortitude. He was also trying various tactics to help me get through this phase, but none of them were really working.

He tried humour. He watched me rush to the bathroom for the fourth time in a day and while I was puking, he called out to me through the door, 'Y, it may be easier if you stop eating and just throw all your meals directly into the toilet. What do you say?' His grin faded when I opened the door, leaned against the doorway with one hand on my hip and fixed him with my most malevolent stare.

He tried empathy. 'Look, I can only imagine what you're going through …' He was interrupted by my snapping, 'Of course you can only imagine it. After all, your part is *over*. Don't you ever kid yourself into believing that you can even in your wildest imagination *remotely* hope to know how it feels to ...' and I went on for about half an hour while he retired, hurt, after a few attempts at 'But honey ...' and 'Suno toh ...'

As a last resort, he even tried to get me to snap out of it. A few weeks into the pregnancy, when he saw me lying about in a depressed manner after work, he adopted a stern tone. 'Now listen. Enough is enough. Do you really think you're doing anybody any good by moping around like this? You need to snap out of it now. You can't just ...' He paused in alarm when he saw my eyes welling up and I started bawling, 'I *knew* it! You don't love me any more. First you impregnate me and then, when I'm getting fat and unattractive, you turn on me like this.' He immediately backtracked. 'Oh honey, I didn't mean that. I'm sorry ... I was so mean to you ...' And the next two hours went by with him trying to pacify me for his behaviour while I wept inconsolably.

Eventually, he cracked the only formula that would work for the first few, difficult months of my pregnancy. He would respectfully stand back and allow me to rush past him to the loo. He refrained from offering me food directly after I came out pale-faced and red-eyed. He avoided eye contact with me and generally stayed out of the way for at least half an hour before approaching me with a plate and he came fully prepared to have his head bitten off.

It was the best of times. It was the worst of times.

No, it was really only the worst of times.

4

What's Up, Doc?

Being pregnant was turning out to mean plenty of visits to the doctor to make sure everything was coming along just fine.

We had been recommended the name of Dr Kiran Kapoor, who was conveniently located at a large hospital just a few minutes away from home.

Dr Kapoor turned out to be a jolly, fat lady who charged a jolly fat fee. She was a thorough professional, very experienced, highly regarded in the field and well-known across Mumbai – as a result of which, she saw, on average, twenty patients in an hour. While this should give one an average time of three minutes per visit, somehow Vijay and I were always being shortchanged down to two minutes and we always felt cheated of our third minute.

Dr Kapoor had a disconcerting habit of ushering us out of her room almost before we sat down. My third month check-up with her was typical of how each visit was turning out to be.

We entered her office, tired but triumphant after an hour's wait and said, 'Hi, doc.'

Dr Kiran said, 'Oh hulloo …' she checked her appointment book for my name, '… ooo, Yashodhara. How are you?'

I jumped at this outlet being given to me. 'Well, not so good nowadays, doc. I've got terrible acidity …'

Dr Kiran cut me off with a reassuring, 'Oh, that's normal.'

A bit disappointed, I began again, 'Also the nausea is just not letting up …'

Dr Kiran said, 'Don't worry, that's normal.'

After a tiny pause, I continued, 'I've developed this strange stiffness in my calves ...'

Dr Kiran didn't seem to think it was strange. Almost before I had finished speaking, she was smiling reassuringly and saying, 'That's completely normal.'

I gave it one more shot and said, 'Okay, doc, but what about my insomnia? Anything I can take for that?'

Dr Kiran said, 'Ya, that's normal.'

After a respectful pause, Vijay said tentatively, 'So, anything she can take for the insomnia, doctor?'

Dr Kiran didn't seem to like this cross-questioning, but she flashed him a fake bright smile and said, 'No, not allowed during pregnancy.'

She then seemed to take our dumbfounded silence as quiet satisfaction with the consultation and dismissed us with an 'Okay? Good. See me after three weeks. Okay? Bye.'

At this point, we found ourselves standing outside her room, the nurse impatiently waiting to collect the consultation fee. Vijay handed over the money reluctantly, muttering to himself, 'Doctor, I want to kill you ... Oh yes, that's normal.'

The only time we did get to spend more than two minutes in Dr Kiran's office was when she got a phone call in the middle of the consultation. We had already noted that she answered her phone every single time it rang. We could understand this – after all, she was a doctor. It could be an emergency.

We waited patiently for her to get off the phone during the fifth-month visit. She finally turned back to us after finishing a fifteen-minute conversation with Sushila, her interior decorator and said, 'Am having the whole house redone, you see. It's such a nightmare. Sushila is really so argumentative. Ha, ha. Okayyyyyy ...' she glanced down at her appointment book '... yyyy ... Yashodhara? So see me after three weeks.'

On the way home, Vijay and I imagined how Dr Kiran might be in the delivery room.

The vision that we conjured up was of her chatting away on her cellphone against a background of screaming and 'push ... breathe ... push!' saying, 'Ya, Sushila? I'm in the middle of a delivery. But don't worry, tell me? The drawing room wall? No, no ...'

It didn't take too much deliberation for us to arrive at the firm decision that when the time came, we would have the baby delivered by a family doctor in Delhi.

There was one particular type of regular appointment that we looked forward to eagerly. It was the ultrasound.

Vivi, who from the beginning had displayed far higher levels of enthusiasm over my pregnancy than I had, was always full of advice on all matters, including the proper ultrasound procedure.

'Tell them to check properly in the ultrasound,' she said knowledgably. 'From all sides. They don't do that sometimes, you know. They have these special high-tech machines, tell them to use those and not the old ones ...' She went on to say something else, but I had stopped listening.

We didn't have to worry about it. The lady who did the ultrasound was a very competent young doctor named Dr Pallavi. She was friendly, she didn't keep us waiting and she answered all our questions. It was sad to think that someday she might turn into someone like Dr Kiran.

At the eight-week ultrasound, we got the first glimpse of

our baby. It didn't look like anything much, but since it was shaped like a peanut, that was how we started to refer to it and the name stuck.

Far more impressive than the first glimpse was the first sound. Dr Pallavi nonchalantly pressed a button and a loud, quick thumping sound filled the room. We looked around in confusion, until the doctor smiled and said, 'And that is your baby's heartbeat.'

Thump-thump-thump-thump it went and my heartbeat quickened in response. Something so concrete, so steady and so *real*, from a tiny peanut-shaped being who weighed barely a hundred grams. Vijay and I exchanged a look and I knew his expression, with its delighted and rather silly grin, mirrored mine.

It was confirmed. There really *was* a baby in there.

Over the next few months, Peanut started to look less and less like a peanut – and more and more like an alien. I was feeling much better and had decided that maybe this pregnancy thing was not all that bad and was finally beginning to visualize a cute baby as the product of all this effort. So I was waiting for the next ultrasound with great anticipation because this was apparently the time when the little creature inside would start to look like a real baby. This was also the time we could hope to go home with a CD with our very first picture of the baby.

However, the baby was not in a cooperative mood that day. First, it kept its hand shyly over its face, only allowing us to get a tantalizing glimpse of a cute button nose. After Dr Pallavi had tried and failed to get a good shot for about half an hour, she sent us off for a while, asking me to come back after eating something sweet. Vijay and I had an ice-cream and a fight about whose nose the baby's resembled more. It got acrimonious, with Vijay resorting to the use of some unkind words to describe my nose. 'Look, I have the cuter nose and you knows it, I mean *know* it. Don't giggle, it was just a slip of the tongue.' Annoyed by my continued laugher, he spat out a rather needless and hurtful 'By the way, your nose looks like a pakoda.'

When we returned, Dr Pallavi said 'Aha. The baby has changed position.' We were happy about this and waited eagerly to see the face. She then informed us that while the baby had changed position, it was now facing my back and this along with the fact that it now appeared to have fallen asleep made it impossible to get the much-anticipated mug shot.

We went home disappointed. I was in a particularly foul mood. After all, I was suffering to make this baby, the least it could do was to oblige us by striking a pose.

Vijay tried to console me. 'Come on, Y. Let's keep things in perspective, shall we? After all, isn't it far more important that this ultrasound showed that the baby is healthy and growing well? Everything is completely normal with your pregnancy and that is something that we should be thankful for. Also, you know there's going to be plenty of time for baby pictures once the baby arrives. So it's really not that bad, is it?'

This earned him a one-minute long cold stare from me, my eyes narrowed into slits.

He phoned to make another appointment for the next day.

Although Vijay had not missed a single ultrasound till then, the next day's appointment was something he had not planned for and he couldn't get time off from work to accompany me.

This visit was more successful. Peanut did a lot of posing, and I got some really nice shots of the baby doing surprisingly human things such as smiling, winking, yawning, digging its nose and punching itself in the face.

Dr Pallavi appeared to be taken with the baby's antics. At one point, she lost her composure and squealed in a manner most unlike her usual calm self, 'Your son's a real cheeky one! He just winked at you.'

I waited for a while and then asked, 'So when you said "son", was that random, or …?'

I hadn't meant to embarass her with this question, because we both knew that she was not legally allowed to tell me the baby's gender – the earlier times that Vijay had tried to weasel it out of her, she had said, 'It's a healthy baby and that's all I can tell you.' But curiosity had now got the better of me, because she had distinctly said 'your son' and not her usual neutral 'your baby'.

She seemed a bit thrown for just a second, but she quickly recovered and insisted that she had just said it unthinkingly, without checking properly.

After she finished the rest of the ultrasound, I thanked her profusely and she wished me all the best. And in her typical cool style, she added in a meaningful tone, 'My mistake, calling it your son. Wouldn't want you unnecessarily painting the nursery walls blue …'

Now, what was that supposed to mean? Had she been right the first time about it being a boy and was she now trying to cover up for her slip? Or was this a subtle helpful hint about it being a girl? I couldn't figure it out but I didn't want to push it, so I just let it go.

Later at home, we discussed it and for some reason, Vijay became convinced that Peanut was a girl. He said he would prove it to me and started to talk to my belly as I lay on the sofa.

He called out lovingly, 'Peea-nut. Are you a boy or a girl?'

There was a ferocious kick from Peanut in response. Vijay realized he would have to change his method of questioning.

He tried again. 'Peanut, are you a boy?' There was no response.

He then went 'Peanut, are you a girl?' This time there was another hard kick.

Vijay looked up at me happily, pleased to have been proven right. I looked back at him sceptically and said, 'Vijay, do you really think Peanut has any concept of what a boy or a girl is? Get real!'

He murmured, 'I suppose you're right.' Then he brightened up.

He addressed my belly again. 'Peanut, can you check and tell me – do you have a pee-pee?'

There was no response.

He beamed up at me, his face the picture of quiet triumph.

The nicest thing about the second trimester was that I was feeling well enough to notice that my husband was pampering me like never before. And since I never said no to a good pampering, this suited me just fine. He carried my bags, offered me chairs, got me the midnight snacks that I requested and even went around the apartment sleepily trying to seal off all possible sources of light when I complained that I couldn't sleep because the room was too bright.

He was concerned to the point of being overprotective. One evening, we decided to walk to the nearby shops to pick up some groceries. Happy to be getting some exercise, I was chatting away animatedly. Vijay was ignoring whatever I was saying, his shifty, alert eyes scanning the road and darting back and forth warily as he tensely shielded me from the oncoming traffic. He even held my hand as we crossed the road, gracefully swinging me onto the non-traffic side.

I was still chattering away when it happened – I lost my balance and started to fall. As if in slow motion, I watched the rough, jagged stones on the street rush up to meet me. But suddenly, the ground stopped moving towards me and I was suspended in mid-air.

For a split second, I couldn't figure out what had happened. I felt like Lois Lane must have when she was plummeting to a certain death from a tall building and Superman decided to intervene and caught her mid-drop.

I looked up at my own personal friendly neighbourhood Superman – my tall, gangly husband towered over me, his face straining with the effort of keeping me semi-upright. He had quickly grabbed my arm and was hanging on with an 'I-will-save-my-wife-and-baby' sort of determined expression. Seconds passed as I hung in that awkward position, unable to either regain my balance or lose it fully.

The problem was that I had just got my underarms waxed two hours earlier. Only those individuals familiar with this particular form of beauty-enhancing self-torture can appreciate how much pain and after-the-event soreness is involved in such an activity. And it was my right armpit that Vijay had now grabbed and was refusing to let go of. In short, it really hurt.

Lois Lane was told reassuringly by Superman, 'Don't

worry, I've got you.' She looked confused and disoriented and asked him the relevant question: 'But who's got you?'

It was a similar situation with Vijay and me, except that I was squealing in agony and my question was 'What's *with* you? Lemme go ... Aaaaahh ...' Finally, gravity won the battle; I slipped out of Vijay's hand, swung around and landed heavily, but safely, on my bum.

I sat on the road, catching my breath. There was absolutely no dignity left in my life any more. But then, if I had to be completely honest about it, there hadn't been much to start with, so I supposed it was okay. At least I had a husband who still didn't seem to care much about my oafishness and was always around to lend that long, helpy-helperton steadying arm.

Eventually, I decided that there wasn't much point to ruminating on life while sitting on a busy road in a highly pregnant state as traffic rushed past, so I allowed my husband to help me up and dust me off. And held his hand the rest of the way.

5

Make Way for Peanut

As difficult as the beginning of the pregnancy had been, the last three months were definitely giving the first three a run for their money. The so-called golden trimester was over and I was huge and uncomfortable, having already gained about ten more kilos than recommended and discovering that simple things like breathing could no longer be taken for granted.

What made things worse was that to our chagrin, for the last trimester, Vijay and I would be living away from each other. Since we had decided to have the baby in Delhi, I would have to move from Mumbai at the beginning of the seventh month because travel after this stage was not recommended. I had a sneaking suspicion that I was more torn up about the prospect of our living apart than he was, though he steadfastly maintained that he would miss me.

As the seventh month began in May, I breezily bade goodbye at work to the various shampoo teams – the local team in India, the regional team in Bangkok and the global team in London. I even cast a silent and respectful farewell skywards to my fictional interplanetary team which I imagined to be located on or at least somewhere near Jupiter. After a surprise farewell party, organized for me by Vivi, during which I gave everyone at work several false reassurances about how quickly I would be back, I went off on my extended maternity leave.

I kept putting off the packing right upto a few hours before I was due to leave for Delhi and then had a panic attack about it. Vijay kindly took over, neatly folding my clothes and tucking them into my suitcase. I watched him and then looked around our home. I would definitely miss this beautiful little pigeon-hole of an apartment. But the fact was, if I were to be completely objective about the situation, it really wasn't big enough for the both of me any more.

One of the things I would miss most about Mumbai was Vivi's company. Despite being somewhat giddy and woolly-headed, she had proven to be a major comfort during my pregnancy and had been second only to Vijay in terms of fussing over me needlessly and offering to carry the slightest of burdens, often even snatching my purse away from me at work despite my protests that carrying half a kilo extra was nothing for my newfound bulk. I had been quite touched. She really was a good friend.

I also knew I would miss my help. As a parting gift, I bought Zarreena a cellphone, a device that she had never owned before and she was thoroughly kicked about it. I also gave Vinod a handsome tip, which he shyly tried to refuse before I pressed it firmly into his hands. I instructed them both to take good care of my husband, which they promised sincerely to do.

As I left to be driven to the airport, Zarreena was all teary-eyed and reached up from her four-foot-two-inch height to give me a hug, extracting the promise that I would be back with the baby soon. When I got out of the car at the airport, Vinod looked at his feet and said in his sing-song, lilting voice, 'Madam, kuchh galati ho gayi toh maafi maangta hoon.'

I was mystified by this and hastened to assure him that he had done nothing wrong, about to add that it must have been Vijay's fault, but I was interrupted by Vijay who explained to me that this was a standard way of saying goodbye in some parts. Strange parts, I thought, as I walked into the airport to leave Mumbai and have my baby elsewhere.

Elsewhere was a place called home. The original Delhi home that I had grown up in. It felt pretty good to be back with my mum and sister.

'The Three Musketeers back together!' I said enthusiastically, over a merry all-girl dinner that the three of us were enjoying after the longest time.

They both agreed how great it was and I started making plans for all the various girly things we would do.

The next morning, I woke up to an empty house. Empty except for me and our old faithful help, Kajal.

'Kahan gaye mama aur Gitanjali?' I asked her.

'Pata nahin,' she said mournfully and then volunteered, 'Roz kaam pe jaate hain.'

Ah. Work. Of course. It was a Monday. Gitanjali had finally decided to stop pursuing higher and higher studies and had actually landed herself a job. And my mum of course, was serving the government until they shoved her out at retirement time. Fine, fine. I could live with that.

I was so bored.

It was incredibly hot in Delhi and there really was nothing to do. There were only so many times you could watch Harry Potter DVDs alone at home. I had thought it would be great to be on leave, but I actually missed a few of the approximately seven thousand people involved with my shampoo brand.

I sat around in my bedroom watching my belly carefully. Peanut was now moving around a lot and I could not only feel it, I could also *see* my belly move with the baby's movements. It was at times like these that I missed Vijay the most. These were special moments that a husband and wife should relish together. Besides, I needed someone to man the camera – it was so hard to take a picture of your own belly, the angle was never right.

I brooded on how much I missed Vijay. I decided I even missed his wisecracks. In Mumbai, when I sat around like this with my now-too-small T-shirts unable to cover my growing belly, he had remarked that I looked like a rickshaw puller.

'They also sit like that when they feel hot, their banians pulled up over their potbellies,' he had explained.

I had felt my blood beginning to boil at this unflattering comment and had started with 'How dare you compare me to a rickshaw puller while I am in this state …' He had looked a bit panic-stricken but then recovered quickly and decided to go on the offensive, crying, 'What do you mean? Are rickshaw pullers not human? Do they not have feelings? Huh? *Huh?*'

For once, I had been unable to come up with an appropriate rejoinder and had kept silent.

Now, I sighed as I kept a solo watch on my belly. It was a lonely task. And frankly, while belly-watching had been fun to begin with, it kind of lost its sheen when you were doing it alone all day.

Of course, the kicking of the baby was the only thing I thought I would miss about the pregnancy. The kicks had started around the fifth month. At first, I wasn't sure what they were – it wasn't clear to me whether it was a baby kicking or just some strange new pregnancy-related gastro-intestinal phenomenon. Then one fine day, it had become unmistakable. The baby was kicking – the actual, real little person inside me was beginning to assert its individuality. When the movements became visible, it caused no end of amusement for a month or so because Vijay and I found we could get Peanut to kick in response to some stimulation. Every time we felt bored, we would give my belly a bit of a poke and say loudly, 'Hey Peeea-nut! Wake up!' and then have a good laugh at the gymnastics that invariably followed.

Around that time, my mother and sister had paid us a visit in Mumbai and they were slightly concerned when we did this for their benefit. 'Come on, Peanut,' I had hollered, poking roughly at my belly. 'Show nani and masi what you can do.'

We had only stopped doing this when Gitanjali drily pointed out that Vijay and I were clearly going to be the sort of parents who would put their child in the middle of a crowded drawing room and coax, 'Beta, aunty ke liye gana gao.' This was a wake-up call – as was my seeing on the 'Life-in-the-Womb' series on National Geographic that sleep deprivation in babies in the womb was not a good idea.

Now, I was treated to a hard kick right in my rib-cage, which took my breath away and had me doubling over or as close as I could get to doubling over, in pain. Apparently the baby was beginning to get its revenge. Sure enough, the kicks got stronger and stronger over the next few days and I started getting whacked right in my rib-cage at around 2 a.m. every morning. I was completely breathless, uncomfortable and sleep deprived.

Even when she was around, Gitanjali was a poor substitute for Vijay. My attempts to get sympathy from her failed miserably. As I waddled around the house with my huge belly, she often sailed past me with minor variations of 'Hey lady. Pass the ball' or 'Quit hogging it. I'm open!'

Another day, she caught sight of my belly and asked with interest, 'What's that dark line?' I said knowledgably that it was the linea nigra – the vertical, dark line that appears temporarily on pregnant bellies. She nodded and then said, 'So is that to demarcate where they're going to cut you open?'

As the due date for my delivery approached, I became more and more frustrated. The doctor had said it looked like I would deliver early, but there were no signs of labour even though I was now officially full term at thirty-seven weeks. My sister archly informed me that since her birthday was around the corner, it would be nice if I could choose to have the baby before or after that date, since she was in no mood to share her birthday. She even remarked that she 'would push it back in if it tried to steal her thunder.'

Her birthday came and went. A few days later, she saw me sitting around, fat and morose and asked flippantly, 'So, no Peanut yet, huh?'

I knew this didn't really warrant a reply but said, 'Umm. No.'

'Lost his way then, has he?'

'Ha ha,' I muttered grumpily.

She then cupped her hands over her mouth and addressed my belly directly. 'Heyy, Peanut ... follow the sound of my voiiiice ... my voiiiice ...'

As I watched her skipping away lightly, the only consolation I had was that one day she would probably be pregnant too. And then, watch out, little sister. Cue diabolical laughter. For now though, my misery was getting no company.

It helped that Vijay visited me every weekend. I looked forward to these visits immensely and often chattered away like a monkey late into the night, until I realized he had fallen asleep.

The third weekend, he arrived in Delhi late at night with a viral infection, probably brought on by the excessive travel and tiredness. He was mortally afraid of infecting me, so he turned his back to me, covered himself with all the sheets he could find and fell asleep. I could understand this behaviour, but was disappointed at not being able to cuddle and talk. Early the next morning, he woke up and was coughing away to glory, so I asked Kajal to make him some tea and toast. He drank his tea, ate his toast and took his morning dose of medicine – and then instead of talking to me, turned his back on me and pulled all the sheets over his head again. I then spent a pleasant ten minutes kicking him on his backside at half-minute intervals, declaring that Peanut had asked me to 'pass it on with no returns.' I knew I was being childish but could not help it. Vijay just lay there quietly for a while, so I convinced myself that perhaps he liked it. It was only when he began to cough again that I stopped kicking.

There were a couple of weekends in the eighth month that Vijay missed coming to visit me because he had to travel abroad for work.

I had once read a quote somewhere that said 'A husband is somebody who wishes he was having half as much fun on his business trips as his wife thinks he is.' It applied to us perfectly.

I remarked sardonically that, when Vijay was taking up the wonderful rural initiative that he was now heading, I had no idea that the US and Europe would be a part of his rural India beat. Explaining that he had to give lectures at various academies because there was so much interest in the Base of the Pyramid nowadays, he argued that it wasn't his fault, just a part of his job. I steadfastly maintained that *everything* was his fault, even more so since he had thoughtlessly impregnated me. He tried to make up by shopping extensively for me during these trips – usually maternity clothes that I outgrew before he even gave them to me and chocolate, which I was not supposed to binge on.

While he was on one of these trips, at the Hague, I felt unusually uncomfortable. Peanut was kicking my lungs viciously and I was barely able to breathe. I was still awake at 1 a.m. after hours of tossing and turning. I knew it was only 9.30 p.m. where he was, so I gave Vijay a call.

He answered with a muffled, 'Huwoo.' My immediate suspicion was that it was due to his guzzling beer. I snapped at him, 'Where are you?'

Vijay sounded like he was in a very good mood. 'I am at the beach!'

'At nine thirty in the night?'

'Oh yes,' he said enthusiastically. 'There's still sunlight over here. Amazing, isn't it?'

I was unimpressed 'Oh, very. So what are you doing?'

'Having a beer and pizza with a couple of people.'

I gave him my best stony silence. He finally realized something was amiss, as he now remembered having said goodnight to me several hours ago. 'What happened? You okay?'

I gave him the melodramatic sigh of the long-suffering wife. 'I cannot sleep.'

Vijay said, 'Mmm-hmmm.' He was trying to be sympathetic, but the effect was ruined because his voice was muffled by the mouthful of pizza he had just bitten into.

I snapped, 'Okay, fine. Let's do it this way, shall we? You sit on a beach at night in Europe, enjoying your beer and pizza, and I will lie here in complete discomfort, unable to sleep, making *your* baby. Okay? Sounds fair?'

There was a long silence as Vijay manfully swallowed his pizza and tried to come up with an appropriate response to this masterful display of emotional blackmail.

The protest that he finally came up with was admirable. 'But honey! The pizza isn't even that good …'

Yes. That made it all better for me.

Was this pregnancy *ever* going to end?

6

The Peanut Arrives

'No, dear, I don't think it's a good idea for you to be in the delivery room,' said Dr Gouri to Vijay.

My due date was now just a week away and this was probably our last visit to the doctor before Peanut arrived. Our comfort levels with this doctor were much higher than they could ever have been with Dr Kiran because Dr Gouri was an old, old friend of my mother's and had even delivered my sister a couple of decades earlier. However, she seemed firm about not letting Vijay be an active participant in the delivery.

Vijay could not conceal his dismay. 'But aunty! I really want to be there and she wants to be there, too.' Before Dr Gouri could point out that it was important for me to be there for my delivery, he corrected himself: 'I mean, she wants *me* to be there, too.'

He looked at me for support and I nodded. Actually, I wasn't so sure I wanted him there because I had recently watched a birthing video as part of my research. It was such a singularly horrifying sight that I suspected if Vijay were present during my delivery, we might just end up celibate for the rest of our lives.

Dr Gouri said, 'Look, I've delivered many, many cases. It's generally not such a great idea for the husband to be there. There's so much blood and gore that some husbands even faint at the sight and I don't relish the idea of having two patients to deal with instead of one.'

Vijay looked affronted at the suggestion that he couldn't hold his own. She went on in a lighter tone, 'In any case, you do realize that she's probably going to be just heaping abuses on you, right? Do you really want to be around then?'

Vijay drew himself up. It was his moment. He said, 'Aunty. If I were to let that kind of thing deter me, I would have left her months ago.'

I scowled while Dr Gouri laughed. He could sense her weakening and said, 'Come on, aunty. I've been practising to be her labour coach. She needs me there.'

Dr Gouri seemed to soften further at this statement. My scowl deepened as I recalled asking Vijay umpteen times to read the 'For the Labour Coach' section of *What to Expect*. Every single time I had opened it to the relevant page and thrust it upon him, I would find him five minutes later with his nose buried in the book – literally, because he would have fallen asleep with it on his face. In fact, the only time he had referred to himself as the coach before this day had been in jest, when he had blown a piercing whistle in my ear and screamed, 'As your coach, I say you go into labour now! And give me forty push-ups while you're at it.'

However, he was looking so beseechingly at Dr Gouri that I could see he genuinely wanted to be with me to give me some much-needed moral support. So I too turned my most pleading smile towards her. She then said that we could 'take it as it comes', but looked more positive about it than before.

'Are you sure you want the epidural?' Dr Gouri asked me as I lay there writhing in the midst of a contraction.

I swallowed the words that were dancing on the tip of my tongue – 'You bet your ass' – and went with the more polite version. 'Yes, aunty – I'm sure. *Please.*'

Since Peanut had refused to come out on the due date, Dr Gouri had insisted on inducing labour. And so, all my worry and preparation about the drill that we were to follow when my water finally broke had been rendered irrelevant. Instead, it was all very planned and after a mere four-hour labour and a lot of screaming, I lay back exhausted. So much for the pre-natal classes in which I had invested back in Mumbai during the second trimester. So much for all the breathing exercises – one short ha, two long hoos – all that had just been hoo-ha in the end.

Absolutely nothing had prepared me for what I had just been through. I'd had no idea how uncomfortable it would be to have that horrible thing called an enema. How disconcerting it would be to be all trussed up in preparation for pushing the baby out, feet trapped in metallic stirrups. And above all, of course, nothing had prepared me for the actual pain, oh the *pain* of labour.

Through all this, Vijay had been by my side every step of the way, holding my hand and diligently noting the timing of my contractions on a piece of paper that he seemed to keep losing every few minutes. In keeping with his usual reaction to stressful situations, he had also lost his command over English and kept referring to them as my 'contraptions'. This, along with various other things, had made me want to hit him over the head with a blunt object, but I had refrained, largely because there had been none handy.

Now Peanut was out and I lay back, with Vijay still holding my hand. He was saying, 'She's so *pretty* … I told you it would be a girl.'

I wanted to tell him that this wasn't the best moment for I Told You So's, but I was too exhausted to speak.

He held out his hands eagerly for the baby and someone batted them away, saying, 'She has to be cleaned first, of course.'

He took my hand again and squeezed it in excitement. Then something occurred to him. 'She isn't crying. Why isn't she crying?' He was now squeezing my hand so hard that despite just having gone through the pain of labour, it made me wince.

'Relax, relax,' said Dr Gouri. She held the baby upside down and thwacked her bottom and sure enough, a series of indignant, piercing wails rang out through the delivery room.

'Okay, are you ready to get the placenta out?'

I gritted my teeth and gave one last push. 'Very good,' said the doctor. It was finally over. My husband leaned over me and ran his hands through my sweaty, tousled hair. I smiled weakly at him and our eyes locked. I could see that he was thinking exactly what I was thinking – how miraculous it was that a whole little *person* that we had created was now here and how incredibly beautiful she was.

He murmured lovingly in my ear, 'Honey, you know what? That placenta is one of the yuckiest things I have ever seen in my life.'

It had finally happened. Vijay was in love with another woman.

We had read that newborns were supposed to be ugly, conical-headed creatures and had steeled ourselves for this, but Peanut was a beauty. Head perfectly round and covered with black hair; fair skin and large dark brown eyes; a cute snub nose which I reluctantly let Vijay take the credit for; and the most perfect little pink lips, the lower of which would quiver heartbreakingly when she cried. Yes, the lips were definitely mine.

Vijay was completely obsessed with Peanut and insisted

on being the one to handle her as much as possible. We were to be in the hospital for four days before going home, while I recuperated and recovered my strength. Vijay happily took complete care of the baby – changing Peanut's diaper, patting her, cooing over her and only handing her over to me for breastfeeding sessions, that too with the utmost reluctance.

I watched him with mixed feelings. On the one hand, I knew it was a wonderful thing that he was bonding so well with our daughter. I was mystified by how he seemed to instinctively know exactly what to do, even though I was fairly certain he hadn't been going around fathering and raising children all over the place. His confidence in most matters regarding the baby made me feel like an inadequate parent, despite all the research that I had done.

But above all, it was like he suddenly just didn't see *me* any more. I tried to push away the thought that it was only while the baby had been inside of me that I had been the centre of attention and now I was being ignored in a way I didn't see myself getting used to in a hurry.

On the second night, Peanut started crying uncontrollably and none of Vijay's attempts to soothe her by patting, rocking or singing were working. I woke up and asked him to give her to me – thankfully, breastfeeding was one thing that had come naturally and with great success to me. The baby was clearly hungry and once I fed her, she calmed down.

But Vijay was having none of it. He was sure that there was something seriously wrong with Peanut. The crying, he said, was not due to hunger, but pain. I asked him how the hell could he possibly know that and he replied enigmatically that he just knew. I then asked him why she had stopped crying after the feed. He looked at me like I was from another planet and explained that it was clearly only a matter of coincidence that the pain stopped when she started feeding.

The next day, he insisted on asking the pediatrician, when he came by on his round, what was wrong with Peanut. I tried not to roll my eyes when Dr Bhardwaj said categorically, 'Nothing.' Vijay impressed upon him that her cries the previous night had been most heartrending. The doctor indulgently smiled and told him not to worry so much – all babies tended to cry – and if it was colic, it would have been for more than the described 'three *continuous* minutes, doc, from eleven fifty-three to eleven fifty-six p.m.'

I could tell that Vijay was on the verge of imitating the cries for the doctor's benefit, so I hurriedly jumped in to explain she had been fine after the feeding. Dr Bhardwaj rolled his eyes to the ceiling and asked Vijay not to observe the baby so closely. Later, Vijay muttered darkly to himself, 'I think we need to get a second opinion, I don't believe this doctor knows much about babies.' He only stopped worrying when he found something else to worry about.

He worried about whether she was feeling too cold and added another blanket. When I tucked it around her, he decided she was feeling too hot and removed it. He made her wear gloves so that she would stay warm and not scratch herself – when she started putting her hands in her mouth, he removed them. He made her wear a hat as recommended by the doctor, but when I did the same, he decided that she didn't like it much, so he removed it. He lamented her long nails and got a pair of nail clippers with a magnifying glass, but didn't have the heart to cut them – after one attempt, he gave up and put the gloves back on again. He would jerk awake at the slightest noise, while the baby slept on peacefully – one late night, he rushed over from the sofa at the other end of the room to check if she was safe, almost tripping and falling on her. I irritatedly asked him how he could confuse the sound of a distant slamming door with that of a baby's cry but he had already tripped his way back to the sofa and fallen asleep again. He was worried about each temporary rash, the little bandages left where they had taken her blood for testing, her umbilical stump and each bout of sneezing and hiccups.

I found myself becoming increasingly resentful about the fact that all we seemed to be doing now was arguing, with Vijay seemingly oblivious to my discomfort – I was feeling completely out of sorts, in pain from the stitches from the episiotomy and still dazed by the overall experience of childbirth. I also found that all my earlier doubts – about our joint capability to bring up a child – had returned in one big flood. She was so tiny and helpless and she cried so much and the two of us could never see eye-to-eye on how to comfort her. It was overwhelming.

As a result of these feelings, the third day after the delivery, I darkly decided that I was suffering from postpartum depression. However, when I informed Vijay of this, he didn't even turn towards me – he only continued to gaze adoringly at Peanut and absently remarked, 'But she is so beautiful. Why would you think about being depressed at a time like this? This is what happens when you read too much.'

My shrieks were apparently heard by Dr Gouri all the way from the other ward and she practically ran over to see what the matter was, while I heaped curses upon every aspect of Vijay's manhood. While Vijay shrank further into his corner, I blubbered incoherently to her about his being such a *man*. She suggested that perhaps a little sedative might be in order, adding reassuringly to him that there was no need to worry, such emotional reactions were normal after the trauma of childbirth and that everything would settle down soon. Neither of us really believed her.

On the plus side, Vijay changed Peanut's diapers with the expertise of someone who did it for a living. A nurse would come by to change her every couple of hours, but he would go along with her to the changing station and do it himself. He would then return with Peanut in his arms, half asleep himself, and inform me, 'Her enconium is still coming out,' before nodding off briefly on the sofa. I deciphered this to mean her meconium, or first bowel movements after birth. Icky dark green stuff. For the moment, I decided to try and enjoy the side benefits of his obsessive behaviour and be thankful that he wanted to be the one soaking up the meconium.

Besides, I hoped that once things settled down a little, everything would automatically get better between the two of us. This was just a phase. Right?

7

New Parents

On the fourth day, I was finally discharged from the hospital. Actually, it wasn't so much a discharge as it was being kicked out. I had shown no signs of wanting to leave – in fact, I was trying to delay our exit as much as possible because the last time I had checked, there were no nurses at my mother's home in Delhi where I would be spending the first few weeks with the baby and this would mean handling the baby myself. But Dr Gouri finally put her foot down, saying, 'Go home now, *please* – it's time to take care of her on your own.'

We headed to my mother's home. Mum accosted us at the doorstep and did the aarti-and-teeka to make sure we had all the blessings we needed. Then we finally got to step in.

I was delighted to find that my mother and sister had done up the guest bedroom nicely, keeping it free from all possible clutter, as per the advice of Dr Bhardwaj. There was even a little picture of Peanut on the wall with the words, 'Welcome Home, Peanut.'

Everyone was delighted to see Peanut, but no one appeared more taken with her than our old-time help. Kajal had been with the family for almost a quarter century and she had taken care of my sister when she was a child. Even now, the fondness that Kajal felt for Gitanjali was unparalleled, but to her slight resentment, my sister had grown up and no longer needed to be chased around with a spoonful of food. So she kept blinking in total adoration at Peanut and saying, over and over, 'Kitna shona baby hain.'

Vijay and I spent a couple of sleepless days at home tending to Peanut and our leisure time mostly bickering about how to handle her. I was slowly getting accustomed to being treated like a prop in the play of life starring little Peanut, which Vijay seemed to think he was directing, but that still didn't mean I had to like it. So when he asked me when I planned to move back with her to Mumbai, I replied coldly that she wasn't even forty days old and they said that a child should not be taken out of the house until it was forty days old. He asked me since when I had cared about what 'they said', but I just haughtily turned away.

'What's wrong with you?' he asked. 'Why are you acting like this?'

I told him that if he didn't know already, there was no point in my telling him, to which he just shook his head a few times. He then repeated his question: 'So when are you going to move back, then? After forty days?'

I was unsure about this. Somehow, I was in no hurry to move back to Mumbai. It was comfortable here, in my childhood home. I thought of our Bandstand flat as claustrophobically small now. Vijay and I seemed unable to agree on anything to do with Peanut and there would be no referee in Mumbai. Besides, I suspected that my mother knew something about bringing up children and it would help me to be around her. After all, she had raised me and my siblings – and I, at least, had turned out just fine. Of course, it was another matter altogether that every time she tried to give me any advice about Peanut, I snapped at her.

Out loud, I told Vijay, 'Why don't you just find good full-time help over there and when that's in place, we'll move back.' He agreed reluctantly that we would definitely need a full-timer and that he would have to begin the search. Nicely done, Y, I thought with great satisfaction, that's putting the onus on him.

Vijay's paternity leave of about two weeks was drawing to a close and he had to go back to Mumbai. He became very morose while leaving, saying, 'She will forget all about me.' He had been valiantly trying to teach Peanut to say 'Papa' although she was only ten days old and made me promise to keep up the efforts.

He left reluctantly and after his first day of work, he rushed home and insisted on trying to do a video chat with us. I finally managed to get the computer set up and he started goo-ing and ga-ing at her. There was some problem with the webcam at his end, however, so I couldn't see him. I figured this would be okay because the point was for him to see the baby but to my surprise, he was very disappointed. He explained that he had wanted Peanut to see him so that she wouldn't forget what he looked like over the next seven days.

I gently tried to explain that as per my research, a ten-day-old baby could barely focus on a hand placed right in front of its face, so it was unreasonable to expect her to look at the computer screen and recognize him on a fuzzy pop-up window. Vijay was unconvinced by this logic. He seemed to think it was all part of a conspiracy to keep them apart.

I realized that while Vijay was away, I would have to learn to change the baby's diapers. I wasn't too confident about doing it myself the first time, so I solicited the help of my sister. Gitanjali firmly held up Peanut's chubby legs, while I did the wiping and the actual cleaning. It took us about ten minutes, but it went smoothly. We were surprised at our proficiency in this exercise and congratulated ourselves.

It was only later, when I decided to change her diaper again, daring to try it alone this time, that I discovered our self-congratulations had been a tad premature. During the earlier round, we had omitted to dispose of the changed diaper and had instead wrapped it up tightly along with Peanut in her blanket. Consequently, she had been lying peacefully, bundled up with an extra dirty diaper for the last few hours.

I quietly tossed the diaper into the bin. I was going to be the worst mother ever.

Vijay locked eyes with Peanut and said in his best Amitabh Bachchan voice, 'Rishtey mein toh hum tumhare baap lagte hain. Naam hain Vijay. Deenanath. Chauhan. Maalum?'

He was happy to be back in Delhi for the weekend so that he could bond with Peanut. The good thing was that during his visits, I could relax a bit since I only had to feed her and Vijay would do the rest. However, any attempt at adult conversation between the two of us still resulted in bickering and unpleasantness. He had a point of view on everything to do with Peanut – ranging from a detailed interpretation of her cries and facial expressions to the diet I should be adopting as a feeding mother. My temper, exhaustion and hormones were getting the better of me and I completely lost it when he tried to give me tips on the most appropriate breastfeeding positions.

We made up only when it was time for the naming ceremony for Peanut. Over the last two weeks, we'd had a series of acrimonious discussions about her name. Every name that one of us came up with was vetoed vehemently by the other. He wanted to go for a 'different' sounding name, whereas I wanted something simple. I had read in an old Reader's Digest once about how when you're naming a kid, just stand at the back door and yell it out because that's how you're going to be using it for years. It seemed like sound, practical advice to me and I could now see why Vijay's family's choice of 'Rama-Shyama-Ajay-Vijay' was eminently sensible, compared to 'Abhimanyu-Yashodhara-Gitanjali'. No wonder my mother had decided to go to work and leave us to the mercy of the maids all through our childhood.

After rejecting many names – including my top contender 'Sunaina', which he said was too old 'and sounds like an aunty's name' and several of his options which he got out of the *Great Book of Hindu Names*, we had finally arrived at a name that we both liked – 'Anoushka'. The daughter of the main character in *Chocolat* was named Anouska and I loved the short version, Anouk; it sounded Indian enough.

My mother had organized a rather sweet little naming ceremony at home but towards the end, the pundit announced that the most auspicious name for Peanut would begin with the sound 'bh'. As the conclusion to the ceremony, Vijay and I were to lean over together and whisper her new name into her ear. All around us, the family was throwing options at us like 'Bhagyashree' and 'Bheemeshwari'. The pressure was on, but a split second before we were to decide, our eyes locked, and in a rare display of complete unity, we leaned over and whispered in a low voice so that only the two of us and the sleeping Peanut could hear: 'Bheemanoushka'.

I was still having sleepless nights. While Vijay had been up almost every night while we were in the hospital with Peanut, at home he lapsed into his usual state of near-comatose sleep. This appeared to have evolved as a self-defense mechanism over the nine months of my pregnancy, when the only way for him to be able to sleep during my most whiny, miserable nights had been to turn his back to me, fall asleep and refuse to wake up despite all my attempts to rouse him.

This deep sleep proved useful to him now, as Peanut woke up almost every two hours, wailing for a feed, a nappy change, or just to be rocked back to sleep. Being a light sleeper, I would get up and handle her needs. In the mornings, I would be bleary-eyed and grumpy while Vijay would be as fresh as a daisy and seemingly unable to fathom why I wasn't all charged up and ready to play with Peanut like he was.

One night, I was awoken by Peanut squirming around and chomping angrily on her fist. I got up and tried to position her properly to feed her before she started wailing and woke up the whole house. She started fussing, crying and wriggling fiercely. I couldn't help but imagine a trifle darkly that she had been some sort of predator in her last life and that's why she didn't let me breastfeed her peacefully – she seemed accustomed to attacking, wrestling and killing her food first.

Eventually, I was victorious, managing to quiet her down and start feeding. It was then that I became aware of a strange sound – a low, rhythmic thup-thup-thup emanating from somewhere nearby. I looked around for the source and saw that it was Vijay.

He had his eyes closed but had stretched out one arm, evidently in response to the baby's crying, and was patting her back to sleep. Except that since she had been with me the entire time, he had actually just been patting her tiny yellow pillow to sleep, with a serene, fatherly expression on his face. I stared at him in bemusement while feeding the now silent Peanut. After a while, he seemed to notice that the crying had stopped. Clearly thinking he had, yet again, done an admirable job in his newly discovered role as Super Dad, he allowed himself a self-satisfied smile, gave the pillow a final loving stroke, slowly pulled back his hand and resumed his peaceful, dreamless sleep.

The following weekend provided a slight variation. Peanut woke up crying and I went through an elaborate routine of about an hour with her – I fed her, burped her, changed her diaper and rocked her back to sleep. By the time I finished this cycle, it was 4 a.m. I finally lay her down between Vijay and me, positioning her to face me. As I was putting her things away, I noticed out of the corner of my eye a familiar hairy arm snaking out slowly from behind her. I turned and saw Vijay had one eye half-open and was sleepily grabbing hold of our baby and turning her over to face him, instead of me, and then patting her back to sleep in this position. I was irritated but too sleepy to bother saying anything, so I just passed out.

The next night, I went through a similar cycle of about an hour while Vijay slept peacefully. Sure enough though, as soon as I lay her down on her side, facing me, Vijay opened one eye halfway and looked straight at her. I was prepared this time and told him pointedly, 'She hasn't burped properly after her feed. The doctor said we should make her lie on her *right* side when this happens.' Having made my point, I turned away to clear her things from the bed. Out of the corner of my eye, I noticed the long, hairy arm reaching out for her again, turning her over to face him, putting her on her *left* side and mumbling sleepily, 'Come on, bitiya, you have to sleep on your right side now – and the right side is always the one where you are facing Daddy. Right?' He patted her lovingly and drifted off to sleep with his arm protectively around her. And I was left holding the dirty nappy.

As I shoved it into the dustbin and got back into bed, I thought about how the differences between us that had seemed so endearing when we first got together now had us bickering like an old married couple. And we had a helpless little creature dependent on us.

God help Peanut.

8

Enter the Kajal

'Honey, don't you think it's time for you guys to move back to Mumbai to be with me?'

It had been three months since we had moved into my mother's place in Delhi. Our initial agreement had been for forty days after Peanut's birth, but I had just ensconced myself at my mother's place and things had been chugging along just fine. I thought I was shaping up to be a pretty fine mother, if I did say so myself. Peanut seemed to be doing fine too – feeding well, growing well, starting to get active and to respond to me in various cooing, smiley and generally endearing ways.

Of course I knew that Vijay wanted to be able to spend more time with her as well and that perhaps it was just a little unfair that in order to do that, he was expected to travel a few thousand kilometres every weekend, instead of seeing her every day when he got home from work. Still, I figured attack was the best form of defence.

'Have you ever considered,' I suggested in response to him, over the phone, 'that perhaps it's time for *you* to move to Delhi to be with us instead? How about that?'

Vijay pointed out that he had a job in Mumbai and that in case I had forgotten, I did too. After my maternity leave ended in a few months, I would have to restart work there. 'Besides,' he said, 'how long can you stay at your mum's?'

'I did it for over twenty years last time,' I pointed out resolutely.

'Dekho, Yashodhara,' he said in his best I'm-the-Man-of-the-House voice, 'as your husband, I command you to come back to your rightful place, by my side ...'

I hung up on him.

Moodily, I busied myself with folding and unfolding some of Peanut's clothes for a few minutes and then paused. I knew he was right, of course. Peanut was growing up fast and he was missing most of it. His weekend flights were taking a toll on him while burning a big hole in our pockets. I was now at a stage where I was confident that I would be able to take good care of my baby. Or at least not harm her too much, given the right level of support.

The support was the only remaining issue. Till now, we had always managed with part-timers, but with Peanut, there had to be full-time help, especially since I would be at work all day. I had heard enough horror stories about evil maids to know that I wouldn't trust just any stranger with my baby.

Still, I knew I couldn't put off moving back for long. As I thought about it, I realized that I actually missed many things about Mumbai – including Zarreena, Vinod and of course Vivi, who had said that she was 'literally dying to see Peanut', which was of course a bit of hyperbole. Yes, it would be good to get back and see everyone there.

If only I could find some good full-time help to take care of Peanut.

I casually asked my mother, 'So, Ma. When are you due to retire?'

She looked suspiciously at me. 'Not for another couple of years.'

'Damn,' I whispered under my breath. Not that it would have been easy to convince my mother to live with us and take care of my baby. She was fiercely independent and for some reason, more socially active than ever, travelling with friends all over the country for mini-breaks every other weekend. I felt a pang of jealousy and comforted myself that at some point, I too would regain my freedom. Just another thirty years or so.

There seemed to be no solution in sight to our full-time help problem, although we had spread the word to all our acquaintances in both Delhi and Mumbai. I told Vijay that until we figured this out, it would be difficult for me to move back, but he wasn't buying it any more.

'But who's helping you there right now?' he asked. 'Mama and Gitanjali go off to work in the morning and come back late in the evening. Kajal is managing the housework. So you're doing it alone right now, aren't you?'

This kind of logical reasoning did not sit well with me. I huffed, 'It's just like you not to understand. It's about moral support also. Besides, Kajal does help sometimes – she watches the baby when I'm bathing and stuff like that.'

It was true. Kajal liked to watch the baby. In fact, she watched the baby a lot.

It had begun from the day that I had brought Peanut home. For Kajal, little Peanut brought back happy memories of the days when my little sister was a baby. I realized now that over the last couple of years, Kajal had become a rather morose and resigned person, not even bothering to moan about her myriad imagined ailments with the same enthusiasm as before. It was only in the last few months since Peanut had been around that there was some sort of brightness in her demeanour. Plus, a couple of days ago she had insisted on showing me some rather unsightly rashes on her left arm, timing it rather well to coincide exactly with my lunchtime. Clearly, the old Kajal was back.

Most weekdays, it was the three of us at home. I would be reading in bed with Peanut in the bassinet by my side. Kajal would be banging pots and pans in the kitchen. But every few minutes, the pots and pans would fall silent and I would look up to see Kajal standing by the door, gazing down at Peanut with a fond expression, looking like a particularly sentimental gargoyle. After a few minutes of this, she would exclaim, 'Kitna shona baby hain' and then reluctantly tear herself away to go back to banging the pots and pans again.

She would sometimes hinder more than she helped. There were occasions when I had managed to make Peanut nod off with a lot of difficulty and was just heaving a sigh of relief when a sudden piercing yell would startle us both.

It would be Kajal screeching 'Kya kar raha hain shona baby? Ohhh … sho raha hain … shorreee!' Of course, Peanut would start crying despite Kajal's immediate apologies and hasty retreat. I would grit my teeth and start the whole routine of putting her back to sleep, all over again.

Still, it was nice to have Kajal around, it made me feel less alone while managing Peanut. However, she was rather underconfident about taking on anything more challenging, like actually holding Peanut – she seemed to think the baby was too delicate, and that it had been too long since she had last held a baby.

I realized that mulling over the problem of good help wasn't really helping. I asked Kajal to watch Peanut while I went for a bath, but I was only about three minutes into the long, luxurious, five-minute shower that I had planned when she knocked on the bathroom door urgently. 'Gudia, Shonee ro raha hain.'

With shampoo in my eyes and unwilling to cut short my shower, I called back to her to pick up the baby and rock her for a couple of minutes.

When I emerged, rubbing my head with a towel, I was greeted by the sight of Kajal holding Peanut. She was indeed a little rusty. She had her eyes closed and was clutching the baby close to her chest, as if afraid she might lose her grip any minute. Her idea of rocking was unique – she would hop on her left foot for a few seconds, before shifting her weight and hopping on her right foot. She was even singing in a low monotone what sounded like some sort of Bengali lullaby – although it could easily have been a prayer to the heavens to help her not drop the baby. Peanut instinctively seemed to know it was best to clutch onto this strange person's sari to avoid slipping off; she was hanging on for dear life, looking rather like a confused little frog.

When Kajal opened her eyes and saw me, she stopped the strange singing and her face broke into a bright grin of pure happiness. She informed me with a note of triumph, 'Maine Shonee ko chup karaya!'

It was then that it first occurred to me that Kajal, who had been with the family for so many years, would be the ideal person to help with Peanut.

But I regretfully quashed the thought – it wouldn't work for a number of reasons.

For one, Kajal was possibly too old for the job. She had been a young woman when she first came to live with us, but now she was close to fifty years of age, although she looked much the same to me as before – her smooth, oiled hair in the perennial braid was still black; she was still a slim figure in her sari; her face, which when younger was already lined with the worries and hardship of her early years before her time with us, had not really aged much further. Still, she was now much slower, and rather inefficient and short-sighted. I knew we required someone much younger and more energetic for Peanut.

Besides, she had been with my mother for so long now that it seemed unfair to think about separating them. In her own bumbling way, she managed all the household work for my mother and sister and was as attached to the two of them as they were dependent upon her. Further, she had not lived anywhere but in this old house for the last quarter century and getting used to living in a new place would be hard on her.

These were the thoughts that ran through my head as I changed Peanut's diaper for what seemed like the tenth time that day. I was dejected as it occurred to me that I was still at square one as far as finding help was concerned. To add to my misery, Peanut pooped on the changing sheet and also managed to soil the onesie that she was wearing. I looked at the mess, sighed and stoically started to change her clothes.

Kajal materialized at my elbow, saying, 'Shonee kya kiya? Poo-poo kiya? Achha ho gaya, poo-poo achha hota hain.' She wisely informed me that this had cleared the baby's stomach. I nodded listlessly and asked her to watch the baby while I went to wash the dirty clothes. Kajal instead grabbed the dirty clothes from me and said that she would wash them. I didn't want to take advantage of her by making her do the dirty work, so I told her she really didn't have to. But she waved me away and trotted off, holding the clothes proudly and called over her shoulder in a gleeful tone, 'Baby ka poo-poo toh mujhe bahut achha lagta hain.'

Her words hung in the air behind her and echoed in my head. She wasn't disgusted by Peanut's potty. She said she *liked* Peanut's potty.

It had to be Kajal.

I sat with my mother, watching as she sipped her evening cup of coffee. I felt a bit guilty about what I was going to ask her. Of course, my mother was the kind of mother who would give you the shirt off her back – except she didn't wear shirts. Despite her generosity, I felt this one favour was too much to ask – she was the one who had brought Kajal from Calcutta so many years ago and she was used to having her do everything around the house.

Then my mother suggested, 'I've been thinking – why don't you just take Kajal with you to Mumbai?'

I was speechless.

She continued, 'I know you think she's too old and slow, but she really seems to love Peanut. And of course, anyone else you get now will be a stranger. Kajal is completely trustworthy – like a member of the family. And she can take a load off you by managing the kitchen while you take care of the baby.'

After a couple of moments, I voiced the doubt that had been bothering me the whole day. 'But how will you manage, Mum? You and Gitanjali are so used to having her around.'

My mother simply shrugged and said, 'Yes. But as they say, your need is greater than ours.'

I swallowed the lump in my throat and said, 'It's perfect, Mum. I should have thought of it myself.'

I threw my arms around my mother, almost knocking her coffee cup out of her hands and narrowly escaped seriously scalding us both.

I asked Kajal later that evening about how she would feel about coming to Mumbai with us. Once she registered what was being asked of her, she reacted with a mixture of surprise and delight. Any qualms that she might have felt about leaving my mother and sister were apparently outweighed by the thought of guaranteed close proximity with her newest little idol. In fact, she seemed very excited by the thought of moving in with us and resolved to help us out in any way possible, saying repeatedly, 'Main Shonee ko itna pyaar karti hoon, oh baba goh!'

And so it was settled. We were finally moving back to Mumbai to be with Vijay. Unsure though I was about how we would reconcile our conflicting parenting styles, we couldn't keep running away from the problem. And maybe my private fear of more proximity meaning more conflict was unfounded – it could actually mean closeness and more understanding. I doubted it, though.

In any case, the days were now filled with a new sense of anticipation.

We were going home.

PART III

! DISASTER ZONE

1

The Homecoming

It was 4 a.m. on a cold day in Delhi. I was woken by little Peanut rooting around for milk. I thought it was just as well, since we had to be up in half an hour anyway for our flight to Mumbai. I fed the baby, thinking about the day ahead.

Vijay had come to Delhi to take us back. As usual, I had a panic attack about the state of the packing just the day before our departure and he had patiently taken over, putting Peanut's and my things together methodically, finishing only late in the night. He had suggested that we get a bright and early start on Sunday morning so that we would have the entire day ahead of us to set things up at home. It had sounded like a good plan then.

At 4.30 a.m., Vijay's phone alarm began to ring. I watched his still, shadowy figure across the bed, as the alarm got louder and louder. He reached out slowly, switched it off and drifted back to sleep peacefully. I waited a full five minutes before calling his name, startling him out of his sweet slumber. I stepped out to go for a bath and noted that the light in the drawing room was switched on. Ah, good, the usually slow Kajal was actually ready, despite her panic about the 'itna kaam, oh baba goh!' that she had to finish before leaving. I went over to check on her and saw her standing in the middle of the drawing room, dressed in a new sari, with her bag packed and ready and a serene look on her face. She looked like she had everything under control. 'Gud mawrning,' she told me sweetly.

I gazed at her for a few moments. Then a sudden suspicion hit me and I demanded to know if she had slept at all.

She beamed at me. 'Bilkul nahin!'

So. I was going to take an airplane ride to Mumbai – with Peanut, Vijay and a sleep-deprived Kajal. It would be an interesting day.

We were at the airport an hour early with our luggage – three full suitcases and Peanut's car seat, along with our hand baggage and of course, Peanut's rocker. Peanut was asleep and I was carrying her in her rocker, covered with my shawl to protect her from the cold. Vijay loaded two trolleys with our luggage and marched on ahead with one, while Kajal struggled with one behind me. I looked back at her, a bit worried.

I had thought that since this was her first flight, she might be a bit nervous, but she had allayed my fears by saying that she had flown before with us when we were mere children, handling my infant sister. Of course, that was over twenty years ago, but she seemed confident enough, so I had relaxed.

Now, as she fought for control over her trolley, which was zig-zagging this way and that, I was not so sure. I asked her to be careful not to run over anyone's feet. She nodded confidently and immediately proceeded to jam the trolley into my shin. I gritted my teeth and trotted on ahead to catch up with my husband.

We got to the counter, in the shortest line for once. Things were looking up, I thought. The efficient Jet employee at the check-in counter processed our tickets quickly and handed us our three boarding passes with a smile. Her smile widened as she saw Vijay playing with the now awake Peanut, then faded as she realized something.

'Sir? *Where is the baby's ticket?*'

Vijay was stunned. 'The baby needs a ticket? Nobody told me the baby needs a ticket! I mentioned so many times while making the reservations that we are travelling with a baby and no one mentioned a ticket! A ticket? Are you sure? Are you sure she needs a ticket? Can't be!'

'Sir, please go and buy a ticket for the baby at the counter outside quickly. There is an infant ticket for some five hundred rupees plus taxes – if I hadn't seen her here, you would have been turned back at the gate.'

'This is ridiculous … no one told me … a ticket! Are you sure?'

The tall, lanky figure raced off, leaving me staring at his back with my mouth open. I couldn't quite believe it. My husband had carefully planned and organized everything with the express purpose of getting our new baby home. And had forgotten to buy her ticket.

I had barely recovered from this when he returned with the infant ticket. Finally, we had everything in hand. I hoped it would all be smooth sailing now.

We were about to board the flight and were proceeding through the gate. I was carrying Peanut and Kajal had insisted on carrying three bags – her own bag, Peanut's diaper bag and my small purse – all tightly under one arm.

As we went through the final security check, the guard casually checked a tag sticking out of the bag most visible under Kajal's arm. 'Ek hi bag hain, na?' Kajal, as expected, ignored this question and trudged past him.

Vijay also ignored the question and the guard lost whatever little interest he had in the matter. It would have ended there, but I blurted out in a bizarre burst of honesty, 'Ek nahin, teen hain.' The guard then called Kajal back and listlessly checked all the three bags – and we found that my purse had not been stamped by the security men at the X-ray counter. Vijay had to go back and get it re-checked, but not before giving me a malevolent glare for opening my big mouth.

In the bus, he looked at me and mimicked in an unfairly high-pitched voice, 'Nahin, nahin! Hamare paas toh TEEN bag hain! Mera naam hain Yashodhara Satyavadi Harish Chandra Lal.'

We finally trudged up the stairs onto the flight and were greeted by perky flight attendants. I was glad that Vijay had at least blocked good seats for us, front row – which meant extra leg space. We got to our seats to find that in this particular craft, the front row seats had hardly any leg space at all, forget anything extra. As an added bonus, there was no window either. We took our seats stoically – I took what would have been the window seat, Kajal was in the aisle seat and Vijay sat in the middle with his long legs encroaching into my already cramped leg space.

The flight was gearing up to take off. And unfortunately, Peanut sitting on my lap was gearing up for a particularly big potty. I could feel her straining and thought, 'Oh no. Not now.'

I had developed a fairly quick, efficient methodology to check whether Peanut had done potty. I would just stick my finger into her diaper. This was perhaps not the smartest thing to do, but it usually worked well. Except when she had actually *done* potty as I now discovered, finding myself unpleasantly potty-fingered.

As soon as the seat belt sign was switched off, I went to the toilet to wash my hands while Vijay changed Peanut's diaper and dirty clothes and Kajal looked on with keen interest.

A few minutes later, I hurried back to my seat to find Vijay dancing in the aisle, rocking a bawling Peanut, who had chosen this most opportune time to throw a massive tantrum. In a few moments, an air hostess came up bat her eyelids at him in the manner that women reserve for fathers of cute, tiny babies and asked him sympathetically, 'Having some trouble, sir?'

In the last few minutes, Vijay had conducted a difficult diaper-changing operation with an uncooperative baby, had undressed her and changed her clothes while she wailed at him like an angry banshee and had then been swaying back and forth like a drunken palm tree in a failing attempt to calm her down.

He replied to the concerned, eyelid-batting air hostess, in his most suave, charming manner, 'No, no trouble at all.'

We discovered that the flight had lots of empty seats. After a while, Vijay sprawled himself across three of them, holding Peanut on his lap. I sat down in the opposite aisle seat, glad that the neighboring seats were also free. The air hostess came with piping-hot breakfasts. I took my own tray and also thoughtfully asked for a north Indian veg meal for Vijay, since he was holding Peanut. As I put his tray down on the table next to mine, the sympathetic air hostess enquired, 'Ma'am is not having anything?' She was referring to Kajal, who was still sitting in her original front row seat. I realized that she was probably feeling too shy to eat, so I asked for another north Indian veg meal for her, which I planned to give to her once the meal trolley passed.

I now had three full meal trays in front of me. I heard Vijay calling my name and turned to see him leaning back in his seat with an amused smirk on his face, Peanut clinging to him like a monkey. He remarked with reproach in his voice, loud enough for a dozen people to hear, 'You know, you're only supposed to take one meal. Don't eat so much.'

I turned red and glared at him, only to get a cheeky grin in return. I waited till the air hostesses passed and took one tray over to Kajal. She was very embarrassed and said, with a touch of emotion, 'Aap mere liye itna sab kya le aaye.' I told her it was a standard airplane meal and asked her not to be shy and just eat. I was actually quite worried that, without any sleep the night before and with the lack of nutrition, she might faint – and that was the last thing we needed.

The rest of the flight passed without incident. Peanut fell asleep in my arms and woke up dutifully to feed just as we were landing. We had reached Mumbai. I reflected that it had been almost six months since I was here last. And then, it had been just Vijay and a grumpily pregnant me who had flown off to Delhi. How things had changed.

We got off the plane and were now inside the Mumbai airport. I went off for a loo break while Vijay collected the baggage. I was very tired. I looked at myself in the mirror and thought, Not bad for a Mum. Not *that* bad, anyway. Just some dark circles under the eyes and perhaps only about ten kilos above my pre-pregnancy weight. I tried not to think about the fact that I now weighed as much as my husband.

Another young woman wafted through the door and stood next to me at the mirrors. She was not only much slimmer and better dressed, but also one of those who managed to have good-looking, straight hair even in humid Mumbai. I told myself that I was a Zen Mother who refused to compare. I coolly finished washing my hands and put my hands under the automatic hand dryer. It refused to turn on. I waited. It still refused. I waited a few more seconds. I could feel the young woman's eyes on me and I muttered, 'Stupid things never work.'

I picked up my bag to leave the loo and noticed she was still looking at me strangely. Too late, the realization hit me that I had been standing with my hands held out imploringly under an empty paper towel dispenser. Feeling like a fool, I beat a hasty retreat. I tried to cheer myself up by telling myself it was just exhaustion, but at the back of my mind I was wondering how I had actually ever managed to gain admission to an IIM. It just went to show – there's no real way to separate the wheat from the chaff and at this point I felt like the chaff of all chaffs. And I wasn't even too sure what chaff was.

2

Back On Bandstand

We collected our luggage and exited the airport. We stood, straining our eyes for our driver until I spotted a familiar car being deftly manoeuvred into a parking spot up ahead at an unnecessarily high speed and a short, thin figure leaping out of the driver's seat in a sprightly manner.

It was none other than young Vinod. I couldn't keep from grinning when I saw him.

Vinod walked up to us, quickly taking the trolley from Kajal and wheeling it to the car. I noted that he seemed to have lost weight since I saw him last. I greeted him, but he seemed tongue-tied with shyness and just smiled at me. I remarked that he had become thin. This seemed to embarrass him even further and he looked down, shuffling his feet. I decided to break the ice and held up Peanut, saying, 'Isko toh hello bolo … iska naam hain Anoushka.' He repeated 'Anoushka' slowly and his face lit up with a smile as he looked at the sleeping Peanut. We piled into the car – miraculously, we fit, despite all our luggage. And then we were off.

When we reached the apartment, the security guards jumped into action and helped us with our luggage. I didn't remember the help in Mumbai being so good. Then it struck me that they would be expecting big tips from Vijay in the khushi of my return with the baby. Well, they would not be disappointed.

I was truly exhausted now and went ahead upstairs, the baby in Kajal's arms. As I fumbled with my key in the lock, I noted a pair of ugly, familiar red-and-yellow slippers outside the door and realized Zarreena must be inside. I applied some pressure to the door with my shoulder and stumbled because she chose to swing it open at the same moment. She yelled at me, 'ABHI ANDAR NAHIN AANA TUMEE!' So we stood there patiently while she squirted a small lemon around us, muttering all the while in a strange little ceremony, which ended with her sprinkling a few drops of water on my feet. And then she grabbed Peanut from Kajal and brought her inside quickly, cooing at her delightedly, if it is possible to coo at the top of your voice.

I introduced Zarreena and Kajal to each other, although neither was listening to me.

Zarreena said, 'YEH TOH SAAB KI DUPLICATE COPY HAIN' and Kajal demurred, 'Wahan pe toh sab kehte hain ki yeh apni mummy jaisi lagti hain.'

Zarreena said, 'OH-HOOO – ISKO TUMNE PAAUN MEIN PAYAL KYON NAHIN PEHNAYA, JEE?' Kajal jumped in before I could answer, 'Hamare yahan haath pe hi pehnaate hain. Paaun pe nahin.'

Zarreena said, 'HAMARE YAHAN PAAUN PE BHI PEHNAATE HAIN!'

Kajal: 'Hamare yahan nahin pehnaate …'

Zarreena: 'PEHNAATE HAIN, JEE!'

I quickly interrupted because I could see this could go on indefinitely. I peaceably suggested that we make her wear payals on her feet sometimes, but not always. Both parties looked satisfied at this and there was a moment of silence.

Then Zarreena said, 'BAHUT SUNDAR HAIN BABA!' and this seemed to momentarily win over Kajal, who looked quite mollified and as proud as if she were solely responsible for Peanut's looks.

After the brief silence, Zarreena seemed to remember something and annouced, 'OH! KITNA KHILONA LAAYA SAAB, DEKHO, DEKHO,' and ran to bring out a large green tub, which she had ingeniously removed from the bathroom to house the toys which I had sent with Vijay the previous weekend. She picked out a musical toy, pressed it to play a tune and told Kajal, 'ISKO DEKHO, BAAJA BAJTA HAIN, JEEE!'

Now, it so happened that the toy she had chosen to show Kajal was one which had been Kajal's favourite back in Delhi. It was a caterpillar that, when pressed on its tummy, played the most annoyingly tinny version of that knick-knack-paddywack song. 'This old man ... he played one ...' Kajal used to play it tirelessly, over and over, with the most adoring smile on her face, to a highly unimpressed Peanut – until I had finally lost patience, confiscated it and hidden it from her. So now, when she saw Zarreena showing it off like a new discovery, it was a bit too much for her. She said, the contempt clear in her voice, 'Mere ko pata hain. Yeh *wahaan* se hi aaya hain. Iss khilone se usko bahut khilaaya hain maine.'

Zarreena was hardly listening, though. She said to Peanut, 'KYA NAAM HAIN? MAINE TOH SONIA RAKHA HAIN ... MAIN SAAB KO BHI BATAYEE ... SONIAAA, SONIAAA, SONIAAAA ...'

Kajal mustered up every ounce of dignity that she possesed and replied in no uncertain terms. 'Mera naam Kajal hain.'

I stifled my laughter but Zarreena cackled unabashedly, 'NAHIN JEEE! ISKA NAAM.'

Kajal said stiffly, 'Achha ... *Iska* naam toh Onoshka hain ...' She considered for a moment 'Par main bhi isko Shonee bulaati hoon ... Shonee ... Shonia ... ek hi hain ...' This similarity over their chosen name for Peanut seemed to make her finally eye Zarreena with approval and they played with the baby quite peacefully from thereon. They were soon joined by Vinod, who had been sent in by Vijay to get further acquainted with Peanut.

While the three of them played, laughed and fussed over the baby, I went to take a look around our little apartment. It looked a lot bigger than I remembered. Vijay had got Zarreena to wash everything, including the curtains, and the whole place looked sparkling new. I walked around the apartment and paused to look at the breathtaking view of the sea. And I suddenly realized that while I would miss the comforts of my Delhi home, I was very happy to be back on Bandstand.

3

Kajal Settles In

Over the next few weeks, we settled back into our life in Mumbai, along with the two new additions to the family – Peanut and Kajal. While Vijay was besotted with the former, there were many things about the latter that drove him up the wall. He had never lived with full-time help before and found it difficult to get used to her – and there was no denying that Kajal definitely took some getting used to.

I personally thought that she was a blessing and was trying to build her confidence in terms of handling Peanut so that she would be able to take care of her when I went back to work. But I didn't want to relinquish most responsibilities just yet, so while I was at home full-time, she really didn't have that much to do for Peanut. She therefore took it upon herself to try and be useful in other household matters. She tended to try too hard to please Vijay and often displayed prize levels of absent-mindedness in her dealings with him. This led Vijay to become convinced that she was out to get him.

One morning, in the first week after we had moved back, she brought Vijay's early morning tea to him, greeting him with a chirpy 'Gud Mawrning, jamai babu!'

Vijay stretched, never at his brightest in the morning. 'Good morning.'

Kajal asked him, 'Biskoot laau?'

Vijay mumbled his assent. 'Haan ... ek, do, le aao ...'

There was a pause, after which Kajal gently repeated, 'Biskoot laau?'

Vijay said a bit more clearly, 'Haan ... ek, do, le aao ...'

Kajal smiled indulgently and disappeared. Ten minutes passed.

Vijay was not usually a biscuit eater in the mornings, but now that the idea had been planted in his head, he was in the mood for a biskoot or two to dunk in his tea and went off looking for the same. He went to the kitchen and found the biscuit tin himself and on his way back, noticed that Kajal was standing by the drawing room window, gazing at the wide ocean in a very contemplative mood. It was as if, he later told me, 'Wo soch rahi thi, main itne bade saagar mein kahaan se biskoot dhoondke laau.' A bit annoyed now, Vijay purposely rattled the biscuit tin as he passed to get her attention.

She turned towards him slowly, the very picture of early morning serenity and proceeded to rub it in with a final, affectionate 'Biskoot laau?'

Kajal also had a tendency to play the martyr in almost every situation. It was an integral part of who she was – I'd had a lifetime to get used to it, but it was proving difficult for Vijay to handle.

One late night, I asked her if she'd had dinner and she looked down at her feet with a little modest laugh and sighed that since jamai babu had not eaten yet, there was no way that she could eat.

This statement, when I repeated it to him, did not please Vijay any more than the title 'jamai babu' did. He had been enjoying his 11 p.m. beer and snack, sprawled out on our sofa.

I suggested that he eat his dinner early so that Kajal, in turn, could eat before midnight, but he became uncharacteristically belligerent. 'Why? Why can't I eat whenever I want to in my own house? Who asked her to wait until I've eaten?' I tried to explain to him that this was how she had always been, but he just grumbled and mumbled. Eventually, he seated himself at the dining table and shovelled down a couple of parathas, but kept glaring occasionally at the kitchen door behind which Kajal lurked.

Vijay was also increasingly convinced that Kajal sneaked around to spy on him, with the singular intent of embarrassing him. Why else, he argued, was it that every time he took off his pants to change into his shorts, she would walk through the door?

Initially, I didn't believe it and thought that he was exaggerating. But then, I saw it a couple of times with my own eyes.

After a hard day's work at the office, Vijay would enter the comfort and privacy – or so he thought – of our bedroom to change out of his pants. Unmindful of the fact that there was now someone else living in our house, he would simply whip off his belt and unbutton his pants, letting them fall in a loose heap around his feet. Exactly at this point the door would bang open and Kajal would walk in with a glass of water on a tray for him. There he would be, frozen like the proverbial deer caught in headlights, his pants trapping his feet, leaving very little to cover his modesty except the length of his shirt and the underwear that always looked tiny at the top of his mile-long legs. Kajal, being short-sighted, would continue to approach him with the glass of water and an ingratiating smile on her face. By the time it became obvious that he was half-naked, it would be too late for her to make a bolt for the door. Vijay would glare at her with his face going red, mutter that he didn't want any water, but then take the glass hastily so that she would just leave.

It was quite fascinating, especially since she never changed the timing of her entrance and he never remembered to actually lock the door. Hence the cycle was repeated at least two or three times a week.

Of course, I pooh-poohed his suggestion that she was doing it deliberately. While I assured him that he might be considered eye-candy by some members of the opposite sex, Kajal was, at over fifty years of age, probably too old for that sort of thing. He continued to eye her with suspicion – and the situation was exacerbated when, one day, she walked in on him in the loo.

This too was due to the fact that he had omitted to lock the door. He had just shut it and settled down for a nice, long bathroom break.

In walked Kajal, slamming the door open with an impressive sense of purpose. Only to find Vijay sitting on the toilet with his pants around his feet and the by-now familiar deer-in-headlights look on his face.

It was, he later blustered indignantly to me, only the fact that he was working on the laptop that saved him from complete and utter embarrassment.

'I'm telling you, Dell ne meri izzat bachha li!'

I nodded sympathetically, but from whatever I had heard, I couldn't agree that his izzat was intact.

One of the household duties that Kajal had assumed for herself was that of taking care of our clothes. Like Zarreena earlier, she would dump various clothes indiscriminately into the washing machine, regularly turning our clothes into attractive shades of pink. She would then hang them out to dry and afterwards cleverly hide them in places where we could never hope to find them without her help. It was clear that she needed to feel needed.

One day, she heard Vijay grumbling after his bath that he could never find his underwear when he needed it. He rummaged around, finally found one at the back of his drawer and got dressed quickly. However, in the meantime, Kajal had also leapt into action. She dove into her secret cove, extracted an underwear and re-emerged to present it to him with a pleased and triumphant 'Chaddi chahiye, jamai babu?'

This by itself would perhaps not have been so bad, considering all that they had already been through together. But at this point, he was sitting fully dressed at the table and having his breakfast. The situation was exacerbated by the fact that the undie in question was actually one of mine and that too a particularly red and skimpy number. He almost choked on his omelette and turned red, mumbling his refusal of her offering.

'What's with her?' he fumed to me later. 'Couldn't she see I was at the table? And giving me *your* underwear! I tell you, she's doing it on purpose.'

I tried to calm him down and stifle my own chuckles. 'Vijay, don't you think you're being harsh? After all, she's an old, conservative woman herself. All this must be hard on her. In fact, she probably gets more embarrassed than you every time.'

He stopped pacing and I saw a wicked gleam in his brown eyes. 'You think? She gets embarrassed?'

I looked at him suspiciously. 'Yes, of course ... What on earth are you doing?' For he had opened my cupboard and was rummaging through the drawers with great determination. He found what he was looking for and held it up – one of the laciest black undies I possessed, a remnant of our honeymoon days. 'There! I'm going to ask her if this is hers!'

The major problem between them, I had concluded, was one of communication.

The fact was that Vijay tended to mumble in the ordinary course of conversation and Kajal was hard of hearing. Therefore, most of his requests escaped her. Further, she was inexplicably shy around him, finding it difficult to talk to him directly, and so would end up addressing the walls instead. I was used to both of their individual eccentricities and thus played the mediator, but it got tiring.

A typical exchange would run thus:

Kajal would murmur to the north-east facing wall in the drawing room, 'Jamai babu ko chai chahiye?'

Vijay, oblivious to having been asked anything, would continue doing whatever he happened to be doing.

I would get a little annoyed at this and say, 'Vijay, Kajal is asking if you want some tea.'

Vijay would look up, surprised. 'When? Where? Oh yes, I want some tea.' He would turn his head to address her over his shoulder. 'Haan, chahiye.'

Kajal would continue lurking behind him, having missed the fact that he had said something to her.

I would grit my teeth and say, 'Vijay, she didn't hear you. You have to speak up, she can't hear very well.'

Vijay would roll his eyes at me and then turn his head all the way around to look at her directly, saying in a clear and penetrating voice, 'Haan, chahiye.' He would then turn his attention back to whatever was occupying him, adding a mumbled 'thank you'.

Kajal, having forgotten the original question but always pleased to be of service, would then ask him, 'Kya chahiye, jamai babu?'

Vijay and she would then look at each other in confused silence. Sometimes I would jump in to clarify things. At other times, I just left the room.

4

The Princess and the Pea-brains

The one thing that Vijay and Kajal had in common was their worship of Princess Peanut.

By the time the baby was about six months old, Kajal was convinced that Peanut was to Superbaby what Clark Kent was to Superman. She believed Peanut had achieved such feats as being able to wipe her own head with her towel when told – 'Sar ponchho!' and brush her own hair with her hairbrush when told – 'Kangi karo!'

The simple truth of the matter, not always obvious to the innocent bystander whom Kajal regaled with stories of Peanut's achievements, was that Peanut's general tendency at this age was to place all objects on her head. So when Kajal handed her a towel or a hairbrush or any such item, she would simply place it on her head. Then Kajal would ask her to wipe her hair or comb it and be delighted by her apparent comprehension.

Still, I was genuinely surprised when I saw that Kajal appeared to be right about the fact that Peanut would actually look down towards her own feet when asked 'Aapke paaun kahaan hain?' She was sitting in her high chair having a meal when Kajal showed me that she could do this. I excitedly told Vijay that I thought Peanut might actually be the genius we had always suspected she would be and asked Kajal to give Vijay a demonstration of this latest achievement. Kajal dutifully said to Peanut, 'Aapke paaun kahaan hain?' and Peanut almost immediately looked down at her feet again. I said, 'Isn't that fantastic?' Vijay nodded drily and then pulled me by the arm to sit on the sofa next to him. He then asked Kajal to get Peanut to give us a repeat performance. As I watched from this angle, it was obvious that when Kajal asked Peanut where her feet were, underneath the high chair tray, she was also unconsciously patting Peanut's feet.

Kajal believed that Peanut fully understood her own name and responded to it. She said 'Onoooshka' and Peanut turned her head towards her. This, I tried to tell her, was just a function of the tone in which one addressed a baby. To demonstrate, I called in the same tone, 'Seth Dhanraj Daulatwaaaala,' and Peanut turned her head towards me. Kajal was unfazed by this, her enthusiasm not in the least dampened.

Kajal would also tell visitors that Peanut could flick her wrist or dance upon being told to do so. This was an interesting trick which I soon figured out. She would actually just watch Peanut closely and whenever the baby spontaneously started to either flick her wrist or wave her arms in the air, Kajal would pipe up with the instruction, 'Aise haath hilao' or 'Dancy karo'. Her sense of timing was so impeccable that our visitors were mighty impressed. The illusion was complete, no one more fooled by it than the doting Kajal herself.

Meanwhile, Vijay continued to try and stake a claim on Peanut as a parent and compete with me for her affections, even more so now that we were living together. He was unashamedly blatant about it, his behaviour bordering on the ridiculous.

One evening, I was sitting and playing with Peanut on the bed. She was in a giggly mood, flopping all over the place and bouncing around on the soft bed. I turned my head for a minute to talk to Vijay and saw out of the corner of my eye that Peanut was doing a backward flop with great gusto. I also noticed simultaneously that my husband had foolishly left his laptop on the edge of the bed, which was exactly where our baby's head was going to land in the next few milliseconds. Time stood still for me, my heart skipped a beat. Some sort of mother's instinct kicked in and without thinking, I lashed out with my right hand and thwacked Peanut's head, deflecting her in the nick of time. She landed safely on the bed, her head narrowly missing the laptop, although her happy four-toothed grin was wiped off her face. Startled by my intervention, she started to cry.

Vijay had so far been a mute observer to this event, but now he leapt into action. To my shock, instead of congratulating me on my quick action, he simply used the opportunity to win some brownie points with Peanut, immediately pouncing upon the wailing, confused child and saying, 'Oh my poor little one … Mama hit you? … Dada ke paas aao … Dada nahin maarega …'

Although Peanut was still young, I fully believed in the fact that she would benefit from our reading to her. I made it a point to sit down with her every evening and read at least three books to her. She obviously understood nothing, but sat quietly, looking at the pictures as I read slowly and carefully, varying the intonation of my voice to keep it interesting for her. I also used the illustrations to point out things that the stories didn't even mention, in order to familiarize her with different objects and concepts.

One evening, when I was too busy to do this, I asked Vijay to take over. He obviously didn't believe in the many benefits of reading to a child, preferring to play with her instead. I insisted that he stop balancing the book on his head and dropping it to make her laugh and actually read something to her. He flopped down on the bed with a sigh, took her onto his lap and started to read the book to her. I was satisfied and went off, but couldn't resist checking after a while to see how he was doing. When I peeped into the room, I saw him flipping through the pages at random and saying, 'Eee dekho … tree … Eee dekho … witch! Eee dekho … bad-tempered bhalu …' He then said, 'Okay, we're done,' and happily plonked down the book and started teaching a giggling Peanut how to do somersaults.

I had a special bedtime song for Peanut. I was very fond of it because it was taught to me by my grandfather. *'Kitni sundar pyaari chidiya … rang birangi nyaari chidiya … aasman mein wo udti hain … phir bhi kabhi nahin dar ti hain.'* This song would take me back to the days of my childhood and fill me with nostalgic happiness – until I heard Vijay lulling Peanut to sleep with it. He had added a unique little twist to my song, replacing the word for 'bird' with the word for 'underwear'.

I had plenty of experience with this tendency of his to spoil songs by changing the lyrics, but hearing him go *'Kitni sundar pyaari chaddiyaan … rang birangi nyaari chaddiyaan'* filled me with great annoyance. It was sacrilege to ruin this, my favourite childhood lullaby. The worst part was that I knew that after this, I would never be able to sing it again without mental images of colourful underwear floating through the sky.

It was still a constant struggle for me to get Peanut to sleep properly at night. She continued to wake up every couple of hours and it was taking a toll on me.

I said wearily to Vijay one day, 'We need to bathe and massage Peanut properly this evening. She may sleep for a few hours then.'

'Sure,' he said. 'I'll do it!'

I corrected him. '*We* will do it. But this time, I think we should reverse the order. We should bathe her first and *then* massage her. It will help her sleep better.'

Vijay made scoffing sounds and said, 'Why? That's not how we do it.'

I asked with interest, 'And who is this "we"?'

Vijay ignored the question and said, 'It just doesn't make sense. See, first we should massage her, then we wash the oil away with a sponge bath.'

I set my jaw resolutely. 'But I've checked – it says everywhere that we should massage her *after* the bath.'

Vijay challenged me on this one. 'And just where have you read this?'

It sounded a bit lame even to me. 'On the Johnson's Baby Oil bottle …' I said. I then continued more confidently, 'But I'm sure I read it elsewhere too. Anyway, it makes sense, doesn't it? A bath is invigorating, a massage is relaxing … so we massage her later.'

Vijay was clearly in an argumentative mood. 'But I always feel sleepy after a bath.'

I said, 'What's wrong with you? Don't you bathe in the morning to get fresh?'

'Bathing only makes you momentarily fresh. I am always sleepy by eleven a.m. in office,' was Vijay's sagacious reply.

I gave him a withering look. 'Hmmm. Don't be so silly, please.'

After a moment of silence, Vijay said, 'Look here, Y. Water makes you tired. After all, don't you feel tired after a swim?'

I asked, the irritation clear in my voice, 'Are you really going to equate a half-hour swim with a five-minute bath in a tub?'

Vijay retreated while I prepared the bath and massage material, both of us now in a sullen mood. A few moments later, he re-entered the battlefield with gusto and played his final trump card.

He spat out, in his I'm-the-Man-of-the-House voice, 'I want one more baby!'

I stared at him, speechless.

He continued, 'And I will do whatever I want, *my* way, with that one!'

It took me a moment to figure out he was just being silly and I couldn't help laughing.

Eventually, we cooperated enough to give Peanut a bath together and the mood was further lightened by Vijay's repeated chanting of 'Har har Gange, Punditji nange' as we poured water on the bemused baby. For the moment, peace reigned in the Lal-Sharma household.

Only for the moment, of course.

5

All Ees Really Not That Well

It was nearing 8 p.m. on Friday. Peanut was already asleep, but Vijay still wasn't home.

I watched the ticking clock, willing the minute hand to move faster. As usual, it didn't work, but it helped to pass the time. I had spent the entire day at home with Kajal and Peanut and was feeling listless and bored.

Many weeks of my maternity leave still stretched ahead of me and I realized that I wasn't cut out to be a stay-at-home mom. It had been nice to sit around doing nothing but staring at Peanut in the beginning, but now a part of me really missed having co-workers to discuss all those important marketing strategies with. And of course, the bitching. Oh, and the coffee breaks.

I craved adult company. However, here I was, stuck at home with only Kajal and Peanut.

I moodily reflected that Vijay seemed to be coming back really late nowadays from work. Sure, he had said he was busy and his office was about one and a half hours away, but that was no excuse. We were rarely getting time together nowadays.

When he came home, all that he was typically interested in talking about was what Peanut had done through the day. Unfortunately, conversations about her would inevitably result in bickering. I thought about how over the last few months – ever since Peanut had come along and especially since we had moved back to Mumbai, our relationship had become more strained than ever. And of late, for some reason, Vijay seemed to be something he had never been before – *cold*.

As I thought about how long it had been since Vijay and I'd had our last proper conversation, I also realized with a start how long it had been since we had actually, uh, done it.

It had been months – I didn't even want to count how many. In any case, I had been suffering some sort of a complex because I was still carrying about ten kilos of extra weight and my piddly attempts at working out were doing nothing to make them go away. But if I had been feeling fat and unattractive before, it was made worse by the sudden realization that my husband evidently thought so too.

This was really the limit. He never wanted to talk to me any more; he didn't find me interesting any more; he never even wanted to *touch* me any more. I grew increasingly agitated at these thoughts.

He had only used me as a mere vessel to fulfil his need to procreate and now that the child was here, I had been relegated to the background as part of the more disposable and movable variety of furniture. I was irrelevant. *Unwanted*. Tears pricked at my eyes as I realized that our relationship was dying, if not already dead.

I would move back to my mother's house for ever, I resolved, only momentarily distracted by a memory of my little sister asking innocently while watching TV at the age of six, 'Why do all women go to Mai-ke when they are angry? Where is Mai-ke anyway?'

The sound of the key being turned in the door brought me back to the present. It was almost 8.30 p.m. I swallowed hard once and blinked back my tears. I really had loved this man. I resolved that even though we clearly were no longer meant to be together, I would handle our impending separation with grace and wisdom.

He strode in, no doubt exhausted after the day's work and long commute, and almost bumped into me as I stood waiting for him rigidly in the hallway.

'Oh, hi,' he said. He was completely oblivious to my state of agitation as he dropped his laptop bag onto a chair and asked, 'What's Peanut doing?'

There was a pause that hung heavy between us as I worked up the strength to compose myself enough to converse with him normally and ask him how his day had been. After all, the key thing going forward would be for us to treat each other with respect. I knew he deserved that much from me.

'I KNOW YOU HATE ME! AND I HATE YOU TOO!' I screamed. The tears began to flow freely down my face as I whirled around and ran into my bedroom, slamming the door shut.

'I know exactly what you mean,' said Vivi, handing me another tissue, which I accepted gratefully through all my unladylike sniffling and snorting. She watched as I blew my nose and continued in a sympathetic tone, 'I'm telling you, all men are alike. They pretend to be so modern, so … you know, metrosexual – but they just don't ever want to talk about anything and they are clearly not in touch with their feelings … or their feminine side …'

As she rambled on, I privately thought that Vijay had never in his life pretended to be either modern or metrosexual – or for that matter, admitted to having a feminine side. But the point about his refusing to communicate was definitely true – now more than ever.

After my little outburst on Friday, the entire weekend had passed with hardly a word exchanged between the two of us. Later that evening, when I had finally stopped sobbing and had let him into our room, Vijay had made some half-hearted attempts to ask me why I had reacted this way to what seemed to him a perfectly innocuous question about our little daughter's well-being. Finally, I composed myself enough to give him the standard explanation that if he didn't already know, there was no point in my telling him. He looked frustrated for a moment but then, to my chagrin, instead of coaxing me to open up and talk about what was really bothering me, he simply shrugged his shoulders and walked away to play with Peanut. I even heard him muttering something like the tamper tentrums weren't cute any more, now that we had a *real* child in the house.

This statement had the effect of hurting my feelings so much that I withdrew completely and barely spoke a word the entire weekend – which really was no mean achievement for me. I only talked to Peanut in a quiet murmur as I breastfed her, assuring her that no matter what happened, I would always love her; that I would do my best to ensure that even after the divorce, her relationship with Vijay would not be impacted adversely despite his treatment of me; that we couldn't forget the fact that he had played a role in her creation, even though it paled into insignificance when compared to what my role as the mother had involved; and that I would never allow her to be unduly influenced by my feelings towards the incredibly insensitive pig that he was. She paused her sucking and looked up at me with strangely intelligent and compassionate eyes, and then proceeded to apply all her might to clamp down hard with her newly sprouted teeth on my nipple, causing me to squeal in surprise and pain.

I knew she was probably just teething, but took this act as an ominous sign that she would take his side in the future. This only added to my misery and so I floated about the house in a mournful and martyred manner – a cross between a depressed zombie and a younger, clad-in-shorts version of that wonderful queen of misery, Nirupa Roy.

In the meantime, Vijay kept himself busy by ignoring me. He was unusually quiet too, showing signs of animation only when talking to Peanut. Even though I lurked in corners, waiting for him to pass by, and made dramatic sounds like melancholy sighs and stifled sobs as soon as I was sure he was within earshot, he just pretended not to hear me and went about his business as if I weren't there.

In all our three years of marriage, this had never happened before.

It was inexplicable.

It was maddening.

And, as I was increasingly convincing myself, it marked the beginning of the end.

And so it came about that now, on Monday morning, Vivi sat by my side on the sofa as I gazed tearfully at the floor. She had taken the day off to be with me – that was just the kind of friend she was. And also, completely unconscientious about her official duties. Still, it was clearly a matter of prioritization. People and feelings mattered more than work to her. Vijay, on the other hand, had got ready in the morning just as usual and gone off to work – not even pausing when I answered his casual 'Bye, hon' with what I thought was a particularly masterful and heartrending goodbye, my voice breaking between the 'good' and the 'bye'. He had just sailed out the door without so much as a backward glance.

'I think,' Vivi said with sudden inspiration, and I stiffened at the tone and these opening words from her because they usually spelt trouble, 'you guys should see a counsellor. I recently ran into an old friend from college – she told me she is a marriage counsellor and practises somewhere in Bandra – her name is Reema and I'm sure she'll be able to help you guys out.' She became more and more convinced about her idea as she spoke. 'I'm going to give you her number. Give it a shot, yaar. You guys are so great together. Don't give up so easily.' The situation was apparently rousing the drama queen buried not-so-deep-beneath-the-surface and she added with feeling, 'A love like yours … could never die.'

As I tried to place the Beatles song from which she had shamelessly lifted that line, I found myself wondering whether it was such a good idea to take advice on serious life issues from someone like Vivi. After all, much as I loved her, I couldn't help but recall her response to my suggestion a few days ago that we all go out on an early morning walk to see the sunrise. She had said with charming logic, 'But the sun rises in the east and we are in the west, na? So how can we ever see a sunrise in Mumbai?' I quashed the memory with the thought that it would be unfair and ungrateful for me to equate a person's understanding of relationships with something as mundane as common sense.

I gathered myself up and looked straight into her concerned face. If counselling was what was required to save our marriage, then counselling it would be.

'I'll do it,' I said, with great determination.

'I'm not doing it,' said Vijay, with great determination.

I had broached the subject when he had come home that evening. Too late, I realized I had sprung it on him with the delicacy of a sledgehammer, getting straight to the point with a cold 'Vijay, I think we must go for some sort of marriage counselling – I've found a number ...' even before he had his first sip of evening tea.

Despite having been a poster-girl for the use of tea to spread harmony in the family, I had made such a rookie mistake. You *never* spring things suddenly on a person after work until they are at least halfway through their evening tea. It just went to show how agitated I was by the whole situation.

While I had expected some amount of resistance from Vijay, I had been unprepared for a point-blank refusal.

'But WHY?' I demanded, despair creeping into my voice. 'Don't you see how bad things have become between us? We don't even *talk* nowadays.'

'Yes, but going to a counsellor? That's like trying to talk through a third party. I think our problems are between the two of us and we need to sort them out ourselves. There's no room for another person in the conversation.'

'But Vivi said ...' The three words were barely out of my mouth before I realized that I had made a tactical mistake. I paused and hoped that he hadn't registered what I had said. After all, it happened often enough on other occasions.

No such luck now, of course.

'VIVI?' Judging by the tone and decibel, he was clearly not happy about this. 'You've talked to VIVI about OUR problems? How could you?'

In panicked self-defense, I blurted out the first thing that occurred to me. 'I didn't say *Vivi*. I said ... Shivi.'

After an incredulous pause, he enquired, 'And who's Shivi, now?'

I sensed that this was not working very well to throw him off-track and quickly abandoned the idea. 'Oh, all right. I said Vivi.' I adopted a more assertive tone, since taking the high ground usually worked. 'Of course I've told her. She's one of my best friends. And it's important for me to have *someone* to talk to – and anyway, it's not as if she wouldn't have figured it out.'

'Vivi,' said Vijay evenly, 'says the sunrise ...'

'Oh, all right!' I cut in. 'That's not the point, though. I think her suggestion made a lot of sense. Why should we not try going to a counsellor? It might help save our marriage.'

'Save our marriage?' he repeated, the note of incredulity thick in his voice. 'You really think that things are so bad that our marriage needs to be "saved"?'

'Of course I do,' I said, surprised by the question. 'You think our problems of the last few months are not serious? We've barely talked all of last week. You think that's healthy? And even when we do talk, it usually results in a fight. And ...'

I noticed that he was now looking thoughtfully out of the window and assumed he was tuning me out. My irritation rising again, I continued, 'And clearly you are not listening, which is only one of the things that really gets to me ...'

He turned back to me with a resigned expression on his face and said, 'Fine, fine. Let's go to the counsellor. Let's "save our marriage".'

I took a deep breath and ignored the sarcasm in his voice. He really was impossible. But at least he had agreed to go with me to Reema.

I silently quoted to myself an inspirational line from a movie, which I wistfully remembered Vijay had made me watch back when we were still a happy young couple.

'I'm okay … I'm fine … I'm feeling better. Baby steps.'

I had never been a Govinda fan, but it made me feel better. Only marginally, though.

6

A Little Counselling Never Hurt Anyone. Much.

Two days later, Vijay and I found ourselves on our way to the counsellor's office. We didn't exchange a word on the way, just carefully observed the scenery outside our respective windows. Vinod, tactful as ever, cranked up the radio to drown out the heavy silence between the two of us.

Reema's office was on the sixth floor of a commercial building. We waited outside her room in a tiny waiting area with two plastic chairs. We had arrived at the appointed time of 6.30 p.m. but there was no sign of anybody else around. We sat down on the plastic chairs and I decided to try and make some conversation.

I murmured, half to myself and half to Vijay, 'The rent here must be a bomb. I wonder why she doesn't just practise at home – doesn't look like she needs much of a set-up for counselling.'

Apparently, he had been thinking along the same lines and had already resolved the question in his mind because he responded almost immediately. 'Maybe she is afraid of being murdered in her bed by the psychos she deals with.'

I hissed at him, 'It's not psychos she deals with. It's people like *us*.'

Vijay chose not to respond.

At that point, the door creaked open and a short, fat, round ball of a woman with thick curly hair rolled in. She stopped when she saw us and raised her eyebrows questioningly.

'Hi, I'm Yashodhara – Reema?'

Vijay added, 'And I'm Vijay, Reema.'

She repeated blankly, 'Yashodhara-Reema? And Vijay-Reema? That's rather unusual.'

This was not an inspiring start and I could feel Vijay's scepticism growing by leaps and bounds. Then Reema seemed to recall something and spoke again. 'Oh yes, of course, of course. We spoke on the phone yesterday. Come in, come in, let's get started. What are you waiting for?'

We had been waiting for her, of course, but I assumed this was a rhetorical question. She ushered us into her office and waved us into the two chairs that were in front of her desk. She rolled behind the desk and sank into her chair, although the difference this made to her height was imperceptible. I noticed that she had terribly thin eyebrows, which made for a strange contrast with the thick hair on her head. She opened a notebook and held her pen poised as if to write. She looked at us expectantly.

We looked back at her expectantly.

The seconds ticked by. Somebody say *something*, I thought, clearing my throat a couple of times. Next to me, Vijay was fidgeting and looking very uncomfortable – just about ready to bolt, in fact.

Finally, Reema seemed to realize that we expected her to open the conversation, and started speaking. 'Okay, then! In this first session today, I'd like to understand the challenges in your marriage, as you individually see them. Just one ground rule – please respect the other person's point of view and do not interject. When it's your turn to talk, talk – when it's your turn to listen, listen. After this, I will draw up a plan based on my assessment of the situation today. Would you like to begin, Vijay?'

She turned towards him enquiringly and he immediately sank lower into his chair as if hoping that by this act, she might somehow miss seeing him there. 'Not really,' he mumbled.

I expected her to turn towards me and ask me to start instead, but she just continued staring at Vijay as if something had just occurred to her.

'Do you, by any chance,' she asked him, 'have a drinking problem?'

While Vijay sputtered indignantly, trying to respond, she added, 'No offense meant, of course. It's just something that I sometimes get a feeling about – call it intuition, maybe – and it's best to check upfront as it helps me to assess the mental health of my patients.'

Vijay looked as though he had a thing or two to say about her intuition, but just answered her in an excessively polite tone, 'No. I do *not* have a drinking problem.'

She continued to stare penetratingly at him and asked, 'Are you sure?'

I realized this was not going very well and interjected on behalf of Vijay, 'Er, Reema, really – he does *not* have a drinking problem.'

She immediately turned to me, as if resentful of my interference and asked, 'Do *you* have a drinking problem?'

I said as evenly as I could manage, 'No. I do not have a drinking problem. *Neither* of us,' I added by way of clarification, 'have drinking problems.' I was only too aware of Vijay stifling an exasperated sigh and quickly said, 'So, could we just get on with the session, please?'

Reema seemed surprised by the suggestion that she was in any way responsible for delaying the progress of the session. She said, 'Of course! So then ... what is the problem with you two?'

I decided to take this opportunity to launch into my well-thought out and articulate speech. 'Well, Reema – the two of us have been married for about three years now. We always knew we had a lot of differences, in terms of background, the families we come from, tastes and so on, and an age gap of almost seven years. But ever since our baby was born a few months ago, we're always arguing about *everything*. Even before that, we had issues – such as he *promised* to quit smoking after marriage but hasn't; and the fact that I sometimes felt he wanted me to put up some sort of act to match up to his family's expectations. But of late, this major distance has crept between us and we're hardly talking any more. We're usually just arguing about something to do with our child's care and upbringing, which is an area in which I was expecting a lot of support from him. I feel that he's being totally insensitive to my needs. On top of which, there is no uh, *romance* between us any more and he doesn't seem to think that it needs to be a priority. I feel lost, lonely, confused and I just can't get him to communicate with me on anything any more.'

Reema appeared to have been listening intently and even though she never broke eye contact with me while I was speaking, her pen was continuously moving and scribbling in her notepad, as if it were separate from the rest of her body. She never even looked down once while turning the page to scribble on the other side and frankly, I didn't see how any sort of coherent note-taking was possible like this. Also, she had been raising her thin left eyebrow at me at regular intervals and I knew that when I was alone at home later, I would be spending a lot of time trying to master this feat.

She finished scribbling a few seconds after I stopped speaking and looked up at Vijay again. 'And what would *you* say is the issue, Vijay?'

Vijay cleared his throat and responded after a thoughtful pause. 'Nothing.'

I could have sworn I heard him add the words 'Your Honour,' under his breath.

Reema, whose left eyebrow and pen had been raised expectantly, lowered both and said, 'Vijay, I may be wrong about this, but I am picking up a sense of reluctance and negativity from you in this session. Is there any reason you feel you can't open up here?'

Vijay looked deeply unhappy about having to actually talk to the counsellor. After clearing his throat once or twice, he finally said, 'Actually, I didn't want to come here at all. I was just going along with her because I thought she would get even madder at me if I didn't.'

I stared at him in disbelieving frustration while Reema said, 'I see. And may I ask why you didn't want to come?'

Vijay answered in a sudden burst of frankness, 'Because I don't think our marriage is falling apart the way *she* does. We only have a few little problems. She's always been like this, getting worked up about the smallest things. It's nothing that we can't sort out ourselves. And I don't believe that some random outsider – er, an *outside party* – should get involved. I find it a little … intrusive, I suppose.'

Reema had been listening very carefully to him, continuously making notes without looking down, but she jumped in at this point to say, 'Oh yes, that reminds me – how's your sex life?'

I watched as Vijay turned a delicate shade of purple. This time I decided I was not going to jump in and rescue him and just waited for him to respond.

He sputtered a bit before answering her, 'Well, *mine* is just fine.' He realized that this statement was not putting him in the best light and hurried to elaborate. 'As in, I know she complains that we don't really ... you know ...' He mumbled a few words incoherently and continued '... often enough, but I really don't know whether it's reasonable to expect that we'll be able to find the time nowadays ... We're both so tired all the time with all the work with the baby around and besides, it's been such an unpleasant atmosphere, so you know ...' His voice trailed off as he ran out of steam.

She finished scribbling her notes with a flourish and sat back.

There was a long pause while she glanced through her notes and then announced, 'So, here is my assessment of the situation. You, Yashodhara-Reema, are clearly an overly dominant personality with self-acceptance issues, who has a problem listening to your husband and understanding his point of view. However, in purely psychological terms, I would say that despite your various mental health issues, you would be considered the more psychologically sound of the two, because you at least appear to be in touch with your feelings – unlike Vijay-Reema here, who has self-awareness and communication issues, is obviously in denial about your problems and has failed to accept the fact that you are both disconnected from each other and obviously headed for a separation, if things are allowed to continue like this.'

She looked at each of our stricken faces in turn and said, 'But the good news is ...' I felt my expression changing to one of hope as she scanned through her notes '… actually, there isn't any good news yet. It's only when the two of you jointly decide that you will be coming for my Twelve Step Relationship Rehabilitation Program that I will be able to help you make any progress on your relationship.'

She leaned forward as much as her ball-like figure would allow and said earnestly, 'Just keep in mind that the happiness of your child depends in large part on your sorting out your issues. Seventy-five per cent of a child's development takes place in the first three years of life. You both should consider that when deciding whether to get the help you need or not. Based on today's session, I have only one piece of advice for each of you. *You*' – she looked at me – 'should attempt to state what you would like as *preferences* rather than demands. And *you*' – she turned to Vijay – 'should seriously attempt to communicate your feelings more, instead of stifling them. That's all for today.'

My head was buzzing with what she had said as she went back to reading her notes. It appeared that she was dismissing us for the day.

Despite her obvious quirks and the fact that my head was spinning, I thought that she was sharp and had pretty much nailed the issues. In any case, the ball was now in our court and we would have to decide whether to continue with her or not. The two of us exchanged glances and then slowly started to get out of our chairs.

'Just one more thing,' she said. We froze.

She kept her pen at the ready and asked, 'Do either of you have a drug problem?'

We were both as silent on the way back home as we had been on the way to the counsellor's. Finally, Vijay spoke.

'I thought that went very well,' he said. I hated that, of late, *he* was the sarcastic one.

'There were plenty of things she got right ...' I began.

'Such as the part about you being more psychologically sound than me, I suppose.' He practically spat out the words, adding in a murmur which he thought I would not hear, 'What nonsense.'

'Well ...' I decided not to go down that path for the time being, although that was exactly what I had been referring to. I changed the subject instead. 'What was with the whole Yashodhara-Reema and Vijay-Reema thing? That was weird.'

'Maybe,' Vijay suggested, 'she thought it was weird that you kept on referring to her as Reema.'

I was surprised 'Why? You think it was too informal? Should I have called her "doctor" or something?'

'That might have been better,' agreed Vijay, 'since her name isn't Reema. I noticed it on the visiting cards she had on her table. They said "Lavanya Aggarwal".'

'*What?*' I squeaked. 'But Vivi told me clearly that her name was Reema when she gave me her number ... She even said they had been friends in college.'

Vijay settled back in his seat with a sardonic smile. 'Only proving yet again that Vivi is the absolute right person to take advice from regarding our marriage.'

I had nothing more to say and we settled back in stony silence.

Vinod thoughtfully cranked up the radio.

7

Guess Who's Coming to Visit?

A couple of days had passed since our visit to the counsellor, whom I began to confusedly refer to in my head as Lavanya-Reema. I had questioned Vivi loudly on the phone as to why she had misled me with regard to her name, but was only rewarded with a gay, tinkling laugh. 'Ah, that's right. Lavanya. I knew it was something close to Reema … what? Well, they both end with "aaa", na?'

I was convinced that going back to her would be the right thing to do for our marriage, but I wanted to give Vijay the time and space to come around to the same decision himself.

'Well?' I planted myself in front of him as he ate breakfast. It had now been three days since our first visit and I'd decided that he'd had more than enough time and space by now.

He paused with his hand midway between his plate and his mouth, his omelette-toast hovering uncertainly. 'Well, what?' he enquired politely.

'Don't pretend you don't know what I'm talking about, Vijay. When are we going back to Reema, I mean Lavanya, to start our sessions?'

'You know what?' he said thoughtfully, 'I don't think I'll be going back there. But all the best with that.'

'WHAT? You want *me* to go for *our* marriage counselling *alone*?'

He winced at the words and said, 'I'm telling you, we don't need counselling. And in any case, I think that counsellor is crazy. Besides, Mummyji and Papaji are coming to visit us next week – what will they think if they find out we're going for *counselling?*'

The tension in the room was suddenly so thick that you could have cut it with a knife. Or I could have just cut it with my tongue, off which the words now rolled slowly and icily, 'Mummyji-Papaji are coming? *Next week?* And just when were you planning to tell me this? When they landed and it was time to pick them up from the airport, perhaps? Or maybe just before they walked into the house?'

Vijay mumbled through a mouthful of toast, but I could make out the guilt in his voice. 'I was going to tell you earlier. I just forgot. I only asked them to come over about a week back.'

'Only a week back, eh?' I said in an overly polite voice. I had never fully understood the phrase 'apoplectic with rage', but I suspected I was getting close to that state now.

'It's been such a cold winter in Jaipur this year.' His tone was more conciliatory now that he realized he had made a tactical error in forgetting to tell me. 'I thought it would be nice for them to come here and be with us in Mumbai for a change. Besides, they haven't actually visited us even once in the three years of our marriage.'

I was silent. This was true. And also, I was thinking, it was a shame that they had hardly had any time with Peanut so far, apart from the flying visit we had paid them over Diwali.

Yes, it would be nice to have Mummyji and Papaji over. It would bring back memories of happier times. And maybe their presence would make for a better atmosphere at home. I hadn't yet told my mother about any of my problems with Vijay, partly due to the fact that it was all just too complicated to explain to her and partly from the conviction that she would take his side, like everyone else in the family. But yes, the way things were, maybe Vijay and I could benefit from some amount of adult supervision.

I took a deep breath and tried to work out some sort of a compromise. 'Look, honey.' He looked up, surprised at the use of the endearment which, I realized, had been missing from our conversations for the past two months. 'I think it will be great if they come here and they should – but I really do think that their being here should not stop us from giving the counselling thing a shot. They don't even have to know about it, we can just go off quietly for the sessions once a week or so. So, consider it a *request* from me.' I paused and swallowed here. I was trying to apply what the counsellor had suggested about re-stating 'demands' as 'preferences' and I hoped it didn't show how much effort it was taking 'We go and see Ree ... Lavanya a few times and work towards sorting out our problems. I know she seemed a little strange, but I would personally prefer it if we didn't give up on it before even starting the sessions. Of course,' I added craftily, 'I can't force you to do it. It's just something I would appreciate, if you think you don't mind giving it a shot, that is.'

Vijay had been listening intently. After a slight pause, he said in an agreeable tone, 'Okay.'

I had to stop myself from doing a double take.

Our erratic counsellor was nothing short of a compact, round ball of pure *genius*.

This was going to work.

I hoped.

8

Hello Ji, Mummyji, Papaji

'What,' I said to Vijay, my hands on my hips in an unconsciously aggressive stance, 'do you think you're doing?'

I had woken up an hour earlier, at six-thirty, but had been drifting in and out of sleep as I lay in bed nursing Peanut. I had been dimly aware of unusual sounds outside our room and once Peanut had fallen asleep again, I had come out to investigate.

All around me, the house was bustling with activity. It appeared that Vijay was spearheading some sort of manic spring-cleaning spree and had assigned various tasks to the team of Kajal, Zarreena and even young Vinod. I took stock: Kajal was pulling down the curtains – presumably to wash them – and trying not to get fully entangled in them. Zarreena was flitting about busily with a bottle of Colin, polishing mirrors and all other smooth surfaces she could see. Vinod was assisting Vijay in clearing out all the junk in order to make more room in the small spare bedroom.

I noted almost immediately that Vijay had apparently classified my drum set in the aforementioned category of 'junk', had dismantled it into barely identifiable pieces and was now in the process of piling the carcass of my hobby into a cardboard box.

I tried to keep my voice steady while I asked, 'Why, *honey*, would you dismantle my drum set without even asking me?'

Vijay had a look of surprise on his face. 'Arrey, the last time you played this was a year ago – it was just taking up space.'

'That's not the point. I *could* have played it. It's just that I've been so busy with Peanut. Maybe I would have started next week. And besides ...' I checked myself before continuing.

'Besides, what?' Vijay asked.

'... besides, you know I have nowhere else to hang my clothes in the house,' I finished somewhat lamely.

Vijay went back to piling the pieces into the box, saying, 'Well, you know you won't be hanging your bras and undies in this room any more while Mummyji-Papaji are staying here. So I thought it would be okay.' He sensed my displeasure and paused. 'You want me to put it back together?'

I said sulkily, 'No. It's okay. It doesn't matter.' I knew he was right and that my percussion instrument was barely used nowadays, except as a convenient clothes line. Still, I thought grimly, he could have *asked*.

Vijay's parents were coming on Monday and that gave us only the weekend to get the house in some sort of order. I decided to throw myself into the fray and get into the spirit of things with some frantic scrubbing. After all, the idea was to make them as comfortable as possible. Also, this would be their first time with us in our home, so it would be nice to make a good impression.

I stepped out into the hall and went towards the drawing room. Just then, Vinod went scurrying past me into the kitchen, his arms full of liquor bottles. As I watched, he dumped his load into a big cardboard box and scurried back towards the drawing room, presumably to fetch the next lot.

I enquired of him exactly what he was doing and why. He said he was following Vijay's instructions. We had to hide all traces of alcohol in the house now that Mummyji-Papaji were due to arrive.

Vijay came out and said, 'Ho gaya? Oh, I forgot about the stuff in the fridge.'

He hurried into the kitchen and took out four bottles of beer and added them to the box full of assorted bottles of whiskey, Bailey's and Kahlua. With one last wistful look at his treasure trove, he told Vinod to hide the box in the storage loft in the kitchen.

I thought this was really going overboard. 'Vijay, why should we hide the fact that we enjoy an occasional drink? We're adults! It's not like we have a drinking problem.'

Vijay looked at me as though I was crazy. He said, 'Well, actually, I don't think my parents are ready for such drastic revelations. It's too soon.'

I couldn't help but snort. 'What do you mean it's too *soon*? It's been three years. So why can't we just live the way that we normally live, even when they are around? Let's show them the real us!'

He protested, 'They already know the real me.'

'So then why do you hide your smoking, drinking and your love for omelettes and chicken nuggets from them? Anyway, I don't think they've ever really had a chance to know the real *me*. I wear shorts at home and pants to work; I read extensively and research the best ways to bring up Peanut; I work out to my exercise DVDs; I play the guitar; I could play the drums *if* they were still around; I eat eggs for breakfast; I like chicken soup.' I became aware that I was entering incoherent, rambling territory and decided to just finish with 'I may be different from your family, but there's nothing *wrong* with any of these things, they're just a part of me. But clearly, you think everything should change to present a different picture to them. Right?'

'Thanks,' he said gratefully. 'That would be great.'

'No, it would NOT be great.' My voice and hackles were both rising. 'You're going to be at work most days, I'm still on leave – it's such a tiny house and it's going to be a strain for me to pretend to be someone else. On top of which, you obviously don't want us to give them even a *hint* of a problem between us, so we have to pretend everything is great. It's going to be like one big act.'

'Come on, Y, it won't be that bad. We all have to compromise sometimes.' His voice took on a soothing quality. 'See, I'm hiding all my cigarettes, aren't I?'

I tried not to clutch at my hair. 'But you already hide those – from me!'

'It's just for a few days. Besides, isn't the idea to make them as comfortable as possible on their first visit? Please, just "kindly adjust"?' He sidled up to me and nudged me in the ribs and slurred, 'Adjusht, pliss? Pliss, adjusht?'

He continued to poke me and after a few moments, I lost my stern expression and almost smiled. I also reminded myself that I had got him to agree to the counselling even while his parents were here. A rather confused metaphor went through my head at this point – something about how I had to learn to pick my battles so that I could win the war in the game of love.

The next day, Vijay went to pick up his parents from the airport while Kajal and I waited at home with Peanut. Zarreena had already left for the day, wringing her hands and praying nothing would go wrong. The frantic clean-up operation had left her thinking that Vijay's parents, whom she had never met, were very strict, conservative and difficult. Despite my reassurances that they were perfectly nice and kind people, I could see that she didn't really believe me.

Kajal suddenly realized that there were six eggs in the fridge and came and asked me, 'Iska kya karein?'

I didn't have a clue. I told her bad-temperedly to dump them in the dustbin.

She rummaged around a bit more and came up with a lone packet of Knorr's Chicken Sweet Corn Soup. 'Aur yeh?'

I said this too now belonged in the bin.

Kajal hovered uncertainly. It was against her nature to throw away any food which was not spoilt. Actually, it was against her nature to throw away even spoilt food and I had to practically ban her from consuming stale leftovers. But then I changed my mind and decided this was my last chance to eat some non-vegetarian food for a while. I asked her to whip up something edible from this raw material while I put Peanut down for a nap.

By the time Vijay returned with his parents, I was feeling a little sick from having gulped down two pancakes, three scrambled eggs and a large bowl of chicken soup. We stood waiting in the hall as the party from the airport arrived – Kajal glowing with the satisfaction of having avoided food wastage and me swaying with nausea, my face a delicate shade of green.

Mummyji and Papaji arrived with just one simple, old-fashioned little grey suitcase. Papaji stood tall at his over-six-feet-two height that Vijay had inherited and as he walked through the door, the house suddenly looked even smaller. Mummyji, tiny in comparison, but eager to see the place, came in and looked around curiously. The first comment she made (to my gratification) was, 'Wah, kitna sundar ghar hain.'

They were very impressed with the ocean view. Vijay threw open the drawing room windows for the full effect.

Peanut then woke up from her nap and cried out and I went to retrieve her from her bassinet in the other room. When I brought her in, there was a touching little reunion, although a lot more enthusiasm was shown by the doting grandparents than the grumpy baby.

The first two days were nice. Mummyji and Papaji settled down well. Zarreena diffidently did the cooking, avoiding onions and garlic like the plague, and her quickness and efficiency were much appreciated. Kajal tried to edge me out of my role as tea-maker by consistently offering to make a cuppa for Papaji before I could and repeatedly told Mummyji about Peanut and her various superhuman abilities. Peanut herself started getting used to her grandparents and would gurgle happily at them and got treated to the kind of massage that only a dadi can give. Vijay and I were being carefully polite to each other, so that no hint of a problem was evident to his parents.

It was a fine, tenuous balance. The kind that never lasts.

Mummyji, with her keen interest in all things culinary, was always curious about the diet of different people. To this end, she questioned Kajal one evening, while they were sitting in the drawing room, as to what kind of food was usually cooked in my mother's house in Delhi. She had correctly presumed Kajal to be the authority on the subject, given her long-standing stint with my family.

However, Kajal was not taking any chances – she too, like Zarreena, had been impressed by the disposal of all the alcohol and non-veg food in the house for this parental visit and wanted to do her bit to avoid trouble.

So she immediately replied with enthusiasm that my family was the type who would not even dream about touching non-vegetarian food, not even eggs. Why, even onion was sparingly used in our house, she said piously, adding that since she herself had personally done the cooking for a number of years, she would know.

Mummyji was taken aback at this rather extreme response, because it was contrary to her impression so far. She asked, in that case, what type of pure vegetarian food *did* actually get eaten?

This question left Kajal momentarily flabbergasted. Although we had a fair variety of vegetarian food in our diet as well, under pressure she could not think of something safe to say and ended up mumbling in confusion, 'Tamatar.'

Mummyji was even more surprised at this. She repeated, 'Tamatar?'

Kajal seemed to think that backtracking was not an option. Instead of deviating to naming other, more conventional dishes, she proceeded to stoutly maintain that the tomato was amongst our favourite food – very healthy and you could make a variety of different sabzis from it.

Mummyji muttered to herself, 'Tamatar ki sabzi … pehli baar suna hain.'

Kajal assured her that in fact, it was very nice and promised to make it for her at some point during her stay. She then pretended to hear me calling her and said, 'Haan, aa rahi hoon,' and escaped the room.

Something she should have done a lot earlier.

I listened in disbelief as Kajal told me, with no small measure of pride, that she had thrown Mummyji off the dangerous track with regard to her questions about our diet.

'Tumne bola hum tamatar ki sabzi khaate hain ghar pe?'

She confessed that she had.

I asked Kajal, as politely as I could, if she had by any chance lost her mind. She mumbled a barely audible confession about how she had been unable to think of anything else at that moment.

I sighed.

Trying to recall the exact line that summed up the situation, I muttered to myself, 'O what a tangled web we weave ... when first we practise to deceive.'

'Haanji? Kuchh bola aapne?' Kajal's contrite and eager-to-please voice broke into my moody contemplation. I assured her I had not been talking to her.

This pack of lies was so needless. It could never lead to anything good.

And it was all Vijay's fault, of course.

9

Mo' Counselling, Mo' Problems

'So, your in-laws have come to visit you for a month?'

I nodded, watching Lavanya's eyebrows rise as she spoke, the left one as always higher than the right.

The two of us were sitting in her office while Vijay waited outside. He had already finished his session, using only about twenty minutes of the scheduled half-hour. As Lavanya had explained, the way it worked was that every week, each of us would have our individual discussions with her, followed by a joint round-up session. Today was Step One of her personally designed Twelve Step Relationship Rehabilitation

Program. We had just started and I found that strangely, I was getting used to her incessant look-ma-no-eyes note-taking and eyebrow acrobatics.

She prompted me to talk, with a probing question. 'So, what do they have to say about the situation between you two?'

'Well,' I squirmed a little uncomfortably, 'we're actually pretending that nothing is wrong. Vijay doesn't want them to know about it or they would worry. They're kind of old-fashioned, you know, they wouldn't really understand this counselling bit either.' I quickly added, 'Well, I haven't even told my own mum yet. You know how Vijay feels about it being a personal matter ...'

'Hmm, I see,' said Lavanya, although I could sense a note of scepticism in her voice. 'So how are things at home just now?'

'It's really not that bad, I guess,' I began. 'Things are *kind* of peaceful.' I thought over the last couple of days and was silent for a little while and then said, 'Actually, I really do hate putting up an act like this. I think Vijay tries to hide too many things from them about us, the way we live – and especially me. It's different from our visits to their place in Jaipur somehow – I guess those are always short visits around festival time ... but this feels more fake somehow.' For a moment, I considered telling her about the tamatar episode, but dropped it on the grounds that it would require too much explanation of Kajal as a character. Or worse, she might ask me to bring Kajal in for counselling and who wanted to open that door?

I went on, 'See ... the thing is, I've never been the type to cook, manage a house and so on and I feel his parents may not really approve of the fact that in three years, I've made very little progress on these things. I think they also feel I'm a bit clueless when it comes to the baby. I am inexperienced all right, but I try to read up all I can and do the right thing. Still, we're constantly having disagreements about what his family considers my newfangled and westernized concepts versus what I think of as their outdated old wives' tales … but I don't know. Sometimes I think maybe they're right. Maybe I don't know anything. Maybe I'm just not up to their high standards or something. Maybe it was all just one big mistake.'

By the time I finished my speech, I was feeling extremely depressed and sorry for myself. I felt my eyes welling up with tears as I looked beseechingly at Lavanya for the help and sympathy that I deserved and needed at this point in time.

'Hmmm.' Lavanya put down her pen and looked at me thoughtfully. 'You know, everything that you just said …' she began and I was all agog '… sounds to me like a load of *crap*.'

My mouth fell slightly open and it crossed my mind that I had never asked her where she went to psychotherapy school. I was unable to say anything in response. It was unnecessary anyway, because she continued, 'First of all, it's not really about acceptance by *them*. I said this at our first meeting – I think your problem is actually one of *self*-acceptance. If you were truly confident and comfortable with who you are, their explicit approval or disapproval would matter a lot less to you. Isn't that right?'

I thought about it and nodded slowly.

'You're a smart person with many talents; you're going to go back to work soon and you'll be bringing money into the household and it's perfectly all right that you aren't interested in the kitchen. Accept that about yourself and let any criticism in this regard just slide off you – like water off a duck's back, you know?

'Your baby is, what, about six, seven months old? You're still a very new mom and it can be overwhelming. You're doing the right thing by figuring out your own opinion about how your baby should be raised and by and large, you seem to be doing fine. It can be very difficult, coming to terms with your new responsibilities and in fact, postpartum depression is a very common phenomenon, affecting up to twenty-five per cent of new mothers – it seems to me that you've possibly undergone some form of postpartum depression, which you may only now be coming out of.'

I felt like jumping up, rushing out to Vijay, doing my 'I-win-you-lose' dance and shouting in his ear, 'Yess! See? PPD! I TOLD YOU SO.' But I refrained from doing this as I felt it would be inappropriate, given what I had just been diagnosed with.

'However ...' There was always a however. I knew she couldn't have just left it as my being an intelligent, talented, superlative young working mother who was successfully pulling herself out of PPD.

'There are a few things which you should realize. The first being that your husband also has a stake in your baby. She wouldn't have happened without him and so it's unfair to cut him off from decisions regarding her. For the first three months after she was born, your reluctance to move out of your mother's place and let him be a part of his baby's life was perhaps not the best thing to do – it made him feel cut off and alienated. After all, you must always remember that she is as much his as yours.'

I thought about throwing in my usual automatic argument about the fact that she would always be more mine because *he* hadn't been through a pregnancy. But then I thought back to the days of the pregnancy, about how he had been there every step of the way – holding my hand as I whined, trying to enter the bathroom to rub my back as I threw up, making appointments and driving me to them, buying me things, carrying my bags – and yet being forced to duck behind the sofa on the many occasions when I was taking out all my discomfort and anger on him. Although he had never really complained about it, I knew that my pregnancy had been very rough on him.

I admitted to Lavanya, 'I guess I have been a little, uh, *fixed*, in terms of the way I want to raise her. But we can't agree on anything now, ever. I don't know what happened – he was great during my pregnancy. But somehow things changed between us almost the minute Peanut was born – it all started to fall apart.'

'Don't be so dramatic.' Lavanya's stern tone made me jump. She continued, 'Nothing started to fall apart. The only thing that happened was that his focus shifted. And perhaps he overdid it a little, possibly because he knew he wouldn't get that much time with the baby since you were in Delhi, but that doesn't mean he stopped loving you. In fact,' she eyed me penetratingly and something told me I wasn't going to like what she was going to say next, 'it may be that being so much younger than him, you've sort of been the baby in the relationship and so you were used to all his attention and became a bit resentful about having to share it. Am I right?'

My first instinct was to hotly disagree, but I restrained myself. I knew almost immediately that while it was a little difficult for me to admit, Lavanya had hit the nail right on the head. I was kind of used to the pampering that Vijay had given me in the good old days, especially the royal treatment during the pregnancy. I realized now that I had expected it to continue after the baby arrived – for him to centre all his attention on me while I took care of the baby. I murmured that maybe Lavanya had something there.

'Well, maybe this is a phase of life which requires a lot more growing up for you,' Lavanya suggested. 'This is a time for *both of you* to focus on and *enjoy* the baby you've made together – and that doesn't mean that you two lose focus of your own relationship. It just means that the equation may need to change now and that's okay. You will be a lot happier if you don't hang on to the past, expecting the same pampering that he's chosen to spoil you with till now.'

I nodded meekly. It kind of made sense, although having to grow up was a sad prospect. Should have thought of that before having a baby, though, I reminded myself.

'Okay,' she said briskly, 'and now coming to the crux of the matter, there is one behavioural change that I had already asked you to make in the first session – to state your desires as preferences rather than demands. Have you been trying that?'

I said, 'Yes … sort of … when I remember. It does help.'

'Good. Keep at it until it becomes a habit. If you act domineering and demanding, it will cause your husband to withdraw further and further into his shell and that is not healthy. The other thing that you need to focus on is treating him with respect and controlling your temper around him. Take deep, even breaths when you feel yourself getting worked up; focus on the fact that the relationship is bigger than the issue; and do not attribute *one* behaviour or shortfall to the *whole* person.'

I thought maybe I should be writing all this down and was about to ask Lavanya for her pen when she looked at her watch and said, 'Okay, that's it for your session. Could you please call in your husband, I would like to talk to you both together now.'

I got out of my chair and creaked the door open. Vijay was sitting there, playing with his phone and pretending that he hadn't been eavesdropping. However, I knew from having been in his place some time earlier that everything that was said in the room was actually quite audible in the waiting area. I gestured for him to come inside. He strode in behind me and we both took our chairs opposite Lavanya and gazed at her expectantly.

'Okay,' she said. 'Today both of you have spoken to me about the problems that you have with each other – I think we're making progress. I've already got a good picture of what is ailing your marriage and with some hard work over the next few months, things may turn around for you. After each session, there will be one simple exercise I will ask you to do as homework.' I felt Vijay stiffening beside me in automatic rebellion at the mention of the H word. 'Just remember that it's a difficult thing to rebuild relationships and it's a process that requires commitment as well as patience. But it's a serious matter and you must remember you've done the right thing by seeking professional help. Do try and focus on each other's positive qualities a lot more.' She looked at us, still grave and unsmiling. 'And please continue to engage in *open* ...' she gave Vijay a pointed look 'and *respectful*,' she gave me a pointed look 'dialogue at home about any issues that may come up and record them if they remain unresolved for our discussion next time. So that's it for today. See you both next we–'

'Wait, wait,' I said eagerly. 'What about this week's homework exercise?'

Out of the corner of my eye, I saw Vijay shoot me an exasperated look, but it was too late for me to take my words back.

'Oh, yes,' said Lavanya as she looked at her watch. She gave a start. 'Already eight p.m.! I must rush.' She quickly snapped her notebook shut, gathered up her papers, picked up her bag and stood. 'Well, it's very simple. The two of you must' – we braced ourselves and she continued – 'go on a date. It is really important for you to spend some time together and try to rekindle your romance. Do it in the next few days. And tell me about it when we meet next week.'

Then she waved absently at us and proceeded to bustle out with her usual rolling gait, seemingly unconcerned that she was leaving us rooted in our chairs. On her way out, she slammed her left hand on the switchboard, turning off the lights and fan in one smooth motion, and we found ourselves alone in dark silence.

We slowly rose from our chairs.

My head was throbbing a bit and I was only dimly aware of Vijay saying with his newly acquired flair for sarcasm, 'Have you noticed we seem to be her *only* clients? Hmm … I really wonder why – she's great!'

10

A Birthday to Remember, Even if You Try to Forget

I opened my eyes at about seven-thirty in the morning, feeling a combination of childish excitement and grumpy resentment.

I turned twenty-six today.

I looked at the tiny sleeping infant next to me. Peanut's

pink lips were slightly parted, her cheeks smooth and round, her eyelashes so long that if they had been anyone else's, I would have suspected they were false. She looked like a little doll. 'Well done, Y,' I congratulated myself, not for the first time, for producing such perfection.

I then looked over at the figure asleep on the other side of Peanut. He was all bundled up tight in a mess of blankets, and completely still. A wave of nostalgia washed over me as I recalled how in earlier, happier days, we had a little tradition on my birthday – Vijay waking me up with a cup of tea which he had prepared himself.

I was contemplating in a melancholy frame of mind how I was already a has-been at the tender age of twenty-six, married to a husband who no longer seemed to love me, when a shadowy figure materialized at my side of the bed, causing me to almost cry out in fright.

'Happy Birthday, Y,' said Vijay, holding out a cup of tea.

A swift double-take caused me to surmise that the sleeping figure on the other side of Peanut was actually just a mess of blankets and the person now standing by the bed was in fact the real Vijay. As my heartbeat slowed back to normal, I was touched to see that he hadn't forgotten our tradition. I sat up and accepted the cup of tea and he settled down at the foot of the bed as I started to sip from it. Maybe this would be a good birthday, after all.

'I was thinking,' he said, 'Lavanya said that we should go out on a date. And it's your birthday today – so how about I take you out this evening to a nice place?'

This was getting better and better. We hadn't been on an actual, real *date* in … ages. Well, at least in about the last year or so. 'Sure,' I agreed, the warmth of the tea spreading through my body along with the warmth of hope that perhaps things between us were finally on the mend.

When I got ready and came out of our room, I found that Mummyji had already been at it in the kitchen and she had made the most delicious atte-and-suji ka halwa because it was my birthday. We had a merry breakfast together of alu-parathas and halwa – and for once, I didn't miss my staple diet of toast and omelette.

Mummyji was happy to hear about our plans to go out in the evening and assured us that Peanut would be fine without us and we really should get out of the house together, sometimes. She also presented me with a really nice blue-and-black striped sweater which Vijay had picked out on her behalf. I tried it on and it was a perfect fit. I grinned around at the lot of them, briefly wondering if this childlike pleasure of receiving gifts on my birthday would last till I turned eighty. I hoped so.

Vijay was going off to work, but he promised he would be home early in the evening. He also hinted that he was planning a surprise gift for me and he would bring it with him when he came home.

I wondered what it would be. A new phone? A new guitar? Maybe a nice watch? It didn't really matter, of course.

An iPod?

I was in an unusually good mood the whole day and started getting ready to go out at about 6 p.m. I showered and put on one of my favourite outfits, a green-and-black dress. It was a bit of a squeeze, but after I'd brushed my hair, put on a pair of earrings and a little lipstick, I found I was reasonably satisfied as I surveyed my reflection in the mirror.

At 6.30 p.m., Vijay came home from work and after greeting Mummyji and Papaji and kissing Peanut on her fat cheeks, he signalled for me to follow him into our room. I went along curiously after him and almost bumped into him when he spun around and produced, with a flourish, a large brown paper bag from somewhere on his person. I reeled backwards a bit at his sudden movement and reeled a bit more at the smell emanating from the bag. 'What's this?' I asked.

He had a loving smile on his face. 'It's your birthday gift.'

'Okayyy.' I said, accepting the slightly oily paper bag with some reluctance. As I looked into it, he said in a loud, proud whisper, 'I bought you *kababs*.'

Ah. This was my gift.

The gift of meat.

Great.

'Thanks, hon.' I tried to sound pleased and grateful. 'But I just ate a while back. Besides, we're going out in a while for dinner, right? You didn't have to do this.' I fished out an unidentifiable piece of meat dripping oil and emphasized, 'You REALLY didn't have to.'

Vijay was quite insistent. 'No, but you said that you are tired of not being able to eat non-veg food in your own home. Well, here you are with non-veg food in your own home. So go on now – eat!'

I was on the verge of telling him hotly that he had completely missed my point about letting me be me and that I had not been talking about the kind of subterfuge involved in sneaking a paper bag of kababs into my room, but something in his face stopped me. I took a bite of the kabab. It tasted like greased cardboard. I chewed for a while and then swallowed bravely, mumbling with some difficulty, 'What is this, anyway?'

Vijay said with a touch of reckless abandon, 'Oh, it's the special mixed meat platter from that kabab shop near Toto's – I didn't know which kind of animal you would be in the mood for, so I figured this would be the best – it has everything, even fish I think.'

My stomach was already beginning to churn, but I felt obliged to pick up one more kabab. I looked at it with apprehension, but Vijay was watching me keenly and encouraged me, 'Eat, eat, go on.' I ate.

It was a particularly uncomfortable experience. I wasn't in the mood for kababs, but felt compelled to pretend otherwise. They weren't even nice kababs and I was all too aware of the smell. Also, I knew Mummyji in particular could not stand the sight or smell of non-vegetarian food – and she was in the next room. When I looked up, I saw that Vijay had his gaze fixed steadfastly on me and it suddenly struck me that he expected me to finish the whole bag of kababs in his presence.

I quickly scrunched up the top of the bag and said, 'You know what? I'm going to save this for later. I'll eat it after we come back from dinner.'

Vijay protested that I should eat all the kababs while they were fresh. 'Fresh' was the last adjective I would have applied to them, but I was determined not to hurt his feelings, so I just said, 'Look at the time, we're getting late,' and dropped the bag in a chair near the window. We finished getting ready quickly and headed out for dinner to a nice quiet restaurant at the Taj Lands End.

Dinner was a pleasant affair and we enjoyed ourselves, laughing and talking about trivial things – he told me what was going on at the office, I told him about the various recent shenanigans of Kajal and Peanut that he had missed while away at work. It was nice that it was just the two of us, after what felt like the longest time.

By the time we were ready to leave, we were in a silly mood. We picked up the car from the parking area. Near the exit was a sign that said 'Please Keep Change Ready.' I giggled hysterically when Vijay confused the man collecting the parking fee with 'Bauji, mere trunk mein doosra T-shirt hain. Chalega?'

It was already past midnight when we reached home and everybody was asleep. We carefully crept past Mummyji-Papaji's room to our bedroom where Peanut was peacefully asleep in her bassinet. Kajal, who was sleeping near her, woke up and dragged her mattress off to the drawing room in a daze, presumably to fall asleep again within seconds. We sank into bed thankfully. The mood was just right for some cuddling to round off the evening.

Just then, my nose was assailed by the smell from the packet of kababs and I grimaced in the dark. The smell must have also hit Vijay because he said reproachfully, 'Hey! You didn't finish the kababs! Come on, I'll get them for you.'

I said quickly, 'I really don't want any more, honey.'

He protested, 'But you hardly ate two pieces. There are still ten more to go. I got them for you.'

'I *know* you got them for me.' I hesitated but then decided to be frank. 'Actually, they were not very nice.'

Vijay was silent for a minute and then said in a hurt and accusing voice, 'It's only because you didn't eat them when they were still fresh.'

I resented this remark and thought it would be better to explain. 'They were not fresh even when you brought them in. Look, I appreciate the thought, but I don't think sneakily eating greasy stale food while hiding in my bedroom is the same thing as eating whatever I want freely in my house.'

Vijay was possibly rather nettled by the 'greasy stale food' remark because he said, 'The trouble with you is that you don't know how to enjoy yourself. Tumhe kabab khane se matlab hain ki ped ginne se? Toh khao! Who is stopping you?'

'Arrey, I'm just saying that this is hardly the way that I would like to eat – a silly bag of yucky kababs as a birthday gift which I have to gulp down secretively in a hidden corner of the house. I keep telling you I just want to be myself and it gets to me when you try to get me to hide things from your parents.'

Vijay's annoyance was obviously rising and he responded by imitating me in a high pitched voice: '"Be myself. Be myself." That's all you talk about anymore. You're like a stuck parrot!'

Too irritated to even point out and mock his mixed metaphors, I just turned my back on him to avoid any more conversation.

He must have been in an unusually foul mood at this point because that's when I heard him add in a spiteful hiss. 'As if it's such a great thing to be *you*.'

An icy cold rage crept over me as I registered that my husband had actually said those words to me on my birthday.

He could sense that I was about to explode and reached out to me, hurriedly trying to backtrack. 'That was supposed to be a joke. I was trying to lighten the mood …'

But it was too late.

11

A Fight of Volcanic Proportions

I scrambled away from Vijay, got out of bed and shouted at the top of my voice, uncaring of who might hear, 'You're the biggest jerk on this planet, Vijay!' Adding one or two rude and unmentionable curses, I stormed out of the room, slamming the door behind me with all my might. I was in such a state that I didn't even realize the most obvious and immediate effect of my yelling – that I would startle poor little Peanut, who of course woke up and began to cry.

Through the shut door I could already hear her starting to wail. I wavered for one split second and almost went back into the room, but pride and anger won out and I didn't turn around. 'Bollocks,' I thought. 'Let him handle her for a while, I need to go and cool off outside.' I continued noisily down the hallway and found my way to the door. I fumbled with the latch, my eyes now welling with tears as I realized that there was no way Vijay's parents would not have heard this outburst. It was too late to do anything about it, so I stepped out of the house and stomped down the stairs. The sound of my clunky slippers slapping against each step gave me a strange sort of satisfaction and I stomped even harder down the three floors, all the way to the ground floor, with the angry phat-phat-phat of my slippers nicely amplified and echoing off the walls.

I reached the door at the bottom of the stairs and pulled it open, startling awake the sleeping guard who appeared to be momentarily confused as to whether to salute me or shoot me. The confusion cleared and he went for a clumsy version of the former. Too bad, because at this point, I was itching for someone to try and provoke me, so that I could beat the crap out of them. But this particular guard was one of the more timid ones and he scurried past me across the small complex to open the back gate for which I was headed. Bandstand was just a few feet across the road from the gate and I figured that only a walk by the ocean with a blast of fresh, salty air in my face could cool me down.

I was dimly aware that despite the late hour, there were people about. Late night party-ers, a few amorous couples and some shadier varieties, all of whom I ignored as I stumbled along. About half a kilometre later, I slowed down my pace, my head finally beginning to clear. A sickly feeling of dismay had begun to set in.

I had done exactly what I had resolved not to do – I had looked the gift kababs in the mouth, or something to that effect. The thought was what counted and Vijay had clearly thought that I would be delighted by that greasy carcass bag. It had been wrong for me to let the situation escalate and to barge out of the house as I had done.

His parents would know that we'd had a fight and a big one at that. I knew he would probably be getting questioned by them and was hit by how unfair it was that he was probably struggling to pacify them and handle their worried probing while indubitably dealing with a crying baby. And here I was, waltzing around alone by the ocean. I found myself turning and beginning to walk back towards the house, albeit at a very slow pace.

A little hope began to dawn in the corner of my mind. Maybe his parents had been sleeping really soundly. Maybe I hadn't made that much noise while leaving. Maybe he had successfully quietened Peanut down and was now lying in bed, patiently waiting for my return. Suddenly, I just wanted to go home and make everything all right and I quickened my pace.

That's when I first heard the shouting.

Some major commotion appeared to be taking place. A whole bunch of people were standing around on Bandstand, right in front of my building, shouting something which was incoherent to me from the distance. As I hurried towards them to see what was happening, a group of five or six young men came running towards me. They appeared to be panic-stricken. They were also clearly drunk, given the fact that they were weaving and lurching this way and that and bumping into each other. I sidestepped them all neatly and they ran past me but one of the men, of the bearded variety with long frizzy hair, paused for a second to give me a wild-eyed stare and then yelled, 'Run, aunty! TSUNAMEEEE!'

For a second, I felt my heart sink to the pit of my stomach. Then some modicum of good sense prevailed and I figured that he was obviously too drunk to be taken seriously – why would a bunch of people gather by the ocean if a tsunami was expected?

Smarting slightly from being called 'aunty', I continued to hurry towards the crowd – something was definitely up and it was too close to my home for my liking. As I reached them, I realized that it was mostly, if not entirely, a crowd composed of the people from my building – I recognized a few of my neighbours, including old Mrs D'Costa, who was standing near the back of the group, shivering in her pink nightie. They were all looking up at our building and I could now hear what they were saying.

'Earthquake … earthquake …'

'The building is about to collapse …'

'Good thing the evacuation happened in time ... with these old buildings, you can never tell ...'

'... I had always heard that this part of Bandstand was on a seismic fault ... but never in my fifteen years here ...'

'Did you feel it? Arrey, the pictures almost fell off my wall ... my dining room table was shaking ...'

Earthquake?

My heart thumping, I looked around for the faces of my family, but I couldn't see them anywhere. After scanning the crowd wildly, I went up to Mrs D'Costa.

'Aunty – have you seen my family?'

Mrs D'Costa had been shivering and murmuring prayers fervently with her eyes closed, but she now fixed me with her hazy blue cataracty eyes. It took her a moment to place me and she said, 'Oh yes, my dear ... I'm sure I saw them somewhere ... in fact, our floor was the first to raise an alarm and as soon as I heard, I alerted the building management to evacuate all the other floors too ...' She and I looked this way and that, but neither of us could spot them. She then patted my hand and said, 'Don't worry, child. They will be all right. God will help us through this crisis.' She piously made the sign of the cross.

The sceptical agnostic in me was not reassured by this and I continued my search for them, weaving haphazardly through the crowd. But then a panicked thought hit me despite my attempts to repress it – could this be some sort of divine retribution? My bad behaviour culminating in the loss of my entire family?

I cursed myself for losing my temper and flouncing out of the house – I wasn't even carrying my cell phone with me so I couldn't reach Vijay. Where *were* they? The crowd was now increasing in size – apparently the other buildings had also been alerted and more people were piling out in their nightclothes and gathering around, a safe distance away from the structures which would inevitably collapse.

And then a flash of intuition hit me.

I knew immediately that they were still in the building.

I didn't know *how* I knew, but I just did.

There was no way I would let them perish in a collapsing building. My baby was in there too. With instant steely resolve, I ran towards the gate which was being guarded by the selfsame meek guard who had let me out barely twenty minutes earlier. He looked as if he were going to try and stop me, but I gave him such a withering look that he just cowered and shrank back. Ignoring the shouts of 'Arrey, guard! You fool! Stop her! Stop that girl ...' ringing out behind me, I ran through the gate and within a matter of seconds, was rushing up the three flights of stairs leading up to my home where I wildly imagined that my family members were no doubt trapped behind some sort of collapsed wall or burning door or fallen tree or something of that sort.

Phat-phat-phat went my slippers, echoing again across the empty stairwell and I finally reached the door to my house. I saw that it was not burning so I just pushed it open and went inside yelling, 'Vijay! Mummyji! Papaji!' and sure enough I speedily located at least two of the aforementioned family members. Mummyji and Papaji were positioned at the drawing room window, looking down curiously at the commotion on Bandstand and they turned to face me as I came rushing in.

Mummyji immediately came over to me and put her hand on my shoulder. 'Arrey beta, Yashodhara, tu theek hain, na?' As I looked around in wild panic, I registered what she was saying. They had been worried that perhaps in a fit of anger, I had gone and done something stupid and that's why Vijay had just gone down to see what the crowd outside was gathering for.

I stopped shooting wild, panicked glances around the house to stare incredulously at her for a split second. They were worried that *I* had done something stupid? Here they were, wasting time peering out of the windows of a building which was on its last legs and they thought I was the one going around doing dumb things?

'Mummyji! Papaji! Earthquake! Aap log yahan kya kar rahen hain!' I screeched in my hapless mother-in-law's right ear. 'Peanut abhi tak yahan pe hi hain? Papaji, we have to get out of the house NOW.'

I ran out into the hall and started to rush towards the bedroom where I could see Kajal rocking Peanut in her arms. I was about to yell some more when Papaji's firm but gentle voice cut through my panic as it followed me down the hall. 'Arrey, beta. Koi earthquake nahin hain. Wo toh bas Kajal ki galat fehmi thi ...'

I skidded to a halt to consider this.

Now that he mentioned it, I realized that there was no sign or sound of any earthquake. Everything was still and in its place.

With a flash of sudden, blinding clarity, I realized what had happened.

When I unthinkingly slammed my way out of the house, I had left behind a scene of complete pandemonium.

Inside our room, Peanut was crying uncontrollably, even though Vijay had picked her up and was rocking her back and forth, trying to quieten her down.

Mummyji and Papaji had of course been awakened by all the commotion. Papaji had heard me shouting at Vijay and had caught a glimpse of me as I passed their room and he had immediately got out of bed and followed me. Of course, I was much quicker than he was and had already disappeared by the time he got out the front door. He stood there at the landing for a while, peering down the stairwell, trying in vain to spot me.

Meanwhile, Mummyji had reached the door of her bedroom and was looking up and down the hall, trying to figure out what was happening. She had only heard loud noises, some shouting and became aware that Papaji and I were no longer in the house for some reason.

It was then, at this point, as she stood there blinking in confusion, that Kajal came tearing out of the drawing room and shouted, 'Mummyji, bhookump aaya! Bhookump aaya!'

Poor Kajal had been in deep slumber when she, like the others in the house, had been rudely awakened by my shouting, stamping and door-slamming. Of course, being Kajal, she had immediately jumped to the wrong conclusion.

In a crazy sort of way, Kajal's pronouncement made sense to Mummyji – after all, she had just seen me and Papaji both speedily vacating the premises. As she would explain later, she had thought it rather selfish of us – 'Papaji aur Yashodhara toh bhaag gaye!' – But for the moment, her instinct for self-preservation had kicked in and blocked out other thoughts. And so it was that she took Kajal by the arm and exclaimed, 'Chal Kajal, apan bhi bhagaein!'

Vijay heard this exchange and tried to quell their panic, calling out while continuing to rock Peanut, 'Arrey, Mummy – koi bhookump nahin hain … sirf Yashodhara thi …' But his voice did not make it in time through our closed bedroom door and so Mummyji and Kajal propelled themselves out of the house in a state of great panic. Just outside in the hall, they bumped into Papaji who, giving up on trying to spot me, was heading back into the house.

Mummyji shouted, 'Chalo, aap *ab* kyon ruk gaye? Bhaago ... bhookump hain!'

A confused exchange followed, but eventually Papaji succeeded in quelling their fears and ushered the two shaken ladies back into the house.

Unfortunately, none of them were aware of a third shaken lady, who had been peering at them short-sightedly through hazy blue eyes through the open door of the flat right next to ours, quivering in her pink nightie.

Mrs D'Costa had first been awakened by the sound of some strange vibrating phat-phat out in the landing and had now come out to investigate the ruckus near her front door. Unable to hear Papaji's low-voiced explanation of the actual cause of the commotion, she only registered the panicked, high-pitched voices shouting 'bhookump'. This had been enough for her and she had proceeded to take positive action to save herself and the residents of the entire neighborhood, after a quick fervent prayer for strength in this hour of need to God in his Heaven above.

Now, back in the house and having reconstructed the likely events leading up to the night's fiasco, my mortification knew no bounds. I retrieved Peanut from Kajal and comforted myself and her with some gentle rocking. After a few long minutes, I heard the sound of my husband's voice – he was back. I could only catch parts of the conversation from our room, but I made out that Papaji was informing him that I had already come home. Vijay in turn was telling Papaji what the scene below was about and I cringed when I heard him say, 'I've convinced them to come back in and that there is no earthquake – it wasn't easy, they just wouldn't believe me. Finally, I told them there was just some misunderstanding that the, uh, *baby* of our house started by creating a lot of noise and confusion and someone else must have been playing a prank, spreading panic about an earthquake.'

I carefully placed the now peacefully asleep Peanut on the bed and lay down with her, cuddling as close as possible to breathe in her baby smell. Vijay returned to the room after a few moments and we exchanged a long look. I was expecting him to be angry, but he just looked exhausted and a little bemused. He lay down on the other side of Peanut and we automatically and wordlessly reached for each other's hands. We lay there together quietly for a while, both of us unable to drift off to sleep.

The various sounds in the apartment and outside started to settle down and peace and quiet once again took over the late night hour. I could now make out the distinct sound of the waves crashing against the shore outside. As I sighed at the thought of dealing with all of Mummyji-Papaji's inevitable questions the next morning, I heard Kajal finally turning off the light in the hallway, while mumbling something that sounded like an indignant 'Bilkul bhookump ki tarah tha ...'

12

Bye-bye, Thank You

'So … you're telling me that last night you were mistaken for a *volcano*?' Lavanya's eyebrows were arched so high that I couldn't even see them any more. She had been listening wide-eyed and open-mouthed as I narrated the incident to her. For once, she had actually forgotten to take notes while I spoke, but now she made a wild scramble for her notebook, in order to capture every relevant detail with her pen.

'Earthquake, earthquake,' I mumbled and then felt idiotic about splitting hairs about this. As if it mattered *which* natural calamity it had supposedly been.

'Hmmm,' she said and there was a long pause as she looked at me thoughtfully, tapping her pen against her round cheeks before she finally spoke again. 'You know what, Yashodhara? It is my professional assessment that you might just need to attend an anger management program. Would you like to try my Twelve Step Anger Management Program as a supplement to your existing program?' Her eyes took on a dreamy look 'You would be the perfect case study – a challenge that I could showcase …'

'No, no, actually,' I hurriedly cut in, 'um, in fact, the reason I came by today was to tell you that we've decided that we'll be trying to work things out on our own and that we, uh, don't think we *need* counselling any more.'

Lavanya's eyes almost popped out of her head and her shocked displeasure at this news was written all over her circular face. It fleetingly occurred to me that she looked like she could kind of use an anger management programme herself. She almost barked, 'I see. And why is that?' adding in a tone that sounded a trifle spiteful to me, 'You're only on Step TWO, you know.'

'Yes, yes, we know,' I said, squirming a bit, thinking that I should have insisted that Vijay be the one to break it to her despite my losing the toss. After all, *he* had been the one who suggested we drop the counselling. I should have at least insisted on best of three. Trying to choose my words carefully, I said, 'The thing is, Lavanya – we've now spoken to his parents and they've been really nice and supportive. Er, and of course, *your* advice so far has been really valuable too. We just think that both of us have been a little foolish but we feel that things should get better soon.'

'Oh,' she said with heavy sarcasm. 'Of course. Things always automatically get better on their own, right? Just like that. No need for concerted effort and any form of *time investment* in the relationship under the able guidance of a trained professional.' She snapped her notebook shut abruptly. 'Fine. Good luck to the both of you. I *hope* you're able to work things out. You make a *lovely* couple. That will be fifteen hundred rupees for two sessions.'

I fumbled for my purse and meekly paid up. As I stood up to leave, I had the strong urge to ask her, 'By any chance, do *you* have a drinking problem?' Instead, I just said, 'Bye, and thanks, Lavanya.' Without looking up, she waved dismissively. As I walked out the door, I glanced back once and saw her ripping out the last few pages of her notebook and beginning to shred them to bits.

'Wow. Thanks a ton, Vivi,' I muttered under my breath and got out of there as fast as I could.

Of course, we had to explain to Vijay's parents the events that had transpired the night before.

I had tried to avoid the conversation by prolonging my breastfeeding of Peanut in the morning, until she bit down hard on my nipple and screamed in angry protest. I finally emerged from my room and hurriedly handed her over to the waiting Kajal.

Vijay and his parents were in the drawing room; Kajal informed me that they were waiting to have breakfast with me. I knew this was only an excuse and that they were really waiting to talk to me about the previous night – but there was no avoiding it now. I reluctantly headed over to them, with a last-minute, desperate sort of hope that perhaps acting like nothing had happened would make it all go away. I cleared my throat and cheerily breezed into the room with a 'Good mooorning, Papaji, Mummyji.'

The looks that I received in return made it clear that it wasn't going to work.

Mummyji, in her no-nonsense way, got straight to the point and asked what the matter was. How could we have created such a ruckus; what could be so serious that we had to cause a neighbourhood evacuation and so on. Papaji, in his mild-mannered way, suggested that perhaps they could help in case we had any problems – after all, that's what parents were for.

Vijay decided to intervene at this point, clearly sensing my acute embarrassment from my general demeanour and from the fact that for once, I had absolutely nothing to say.

The gist of his eloquent speech in Hindi was that we had been having some fights lately; a lot of them were to do with how to raise Peanut and in general, about the various differences that we had. And perhaps we had been wrong to hide it from them.

He went on to say that he thought the solution was simple

– for us to accept each other as we were. To my utter surprise, he bravely added that this meant *everybody* accepting that I was not exactly the type of bahu they may have wanted. Avoiding my incredulous eye, he confessed that I had plenty of good qualities and if they were focused on – and if you managed to forget for a moment my tendency to simulate earthquakes – I really was a great person to be with.

He even went on to admit that we had not been honest about the way in which we had portrayed our lives to them – for example, once in a while, we indulged in a drink or two. He hurriedly added that neither of us had any drinking problems, nor did we intend to any time in the forseeable future.

Mummyji had been hearing him out rather impatiently and she jumped in at this point to tell him that she had always known all of this – and that it had never been an issue in the first place. She also said, rather tartly, that it had been hard to believe Kajal's stories about the staple diet of my family being the tomato. Papaji then interjected to point out that all these were just little details and that the most important thing for them was that we try and be happy together.

There was a lull in the conversation at this point and we were all lost in our own thoughts. There was some noise from just outside the doorway and I became dimly aware it was Peanut struggling and squealing to get out of the arms of the clearly eavesdropping Kajal.

Something struck Vijay then and he asked Mummyji and Papaji whether, in their fifty-odd years of marriage, they had themselves had a really serious fight – because as he declared wonderingly, he certainly didn't recall being witness to even small arguments in all his years at home with them.

Mummyji almost snorted and said, 'Ladne ki kya baat

hain? Arrey, kabhi main maan jaati hoon, kabhi wo maan jaate hain.'

Yeah right, I thought. Sometimes I agree with what he's saying, sometimes he agrees with what I'm saying. As if that would solve everything.

After breakfast, Vijay and I went out for a walk on Bandstand. We walked along side by side in silence for a while.

I spoke first and said with complete earnestness, 'I *am* really sorry about last night. You know that, na?'

He looked seriously at me for a moment. I knew there was no reason he should let me off that easily, but then his mouth twitched and he said, 'Why, did something happen last night?' and then he started laughing.

I gazed at him in wonderment, thinking for a moment that perhaps the stress had got to him and he had finally lost it. He put his arm around me and said, 'Oh, honey ... you're such a ... bhookump.'

It was at this point that he told me about the exchange that he had heard between Mummyji and Kajal. He imitated Kajal's 'Mummyji-Mummyji-bhookump-aaya,' and despite my mortification and embarassment, I couldn't help laughing as I pictured the scene. Then we fell silent, content to just walk together.

This time he spoke first. 'Look. We both know that we need to sort things out. But I really don't think it's about counselling. What we need is something more basic, perhaps ... like you not trying to kill me every time I say something you don't agree with ... You being just a little less sarcastic ... And as I said, our being more accepting of each other.'

I reluctantly admitted that perhaps one of the issues we had was my constant flaring up and my liberal use of sarcasm on every occasion. I promised to work on it, but couldn't resist adding, 'You know, you've really added to the stress by trying to turn me into a different person around the family – till that little speech you just gave your parents, which was very nice, by the way.'

'Wasn't it?' He looked pleased 'Well, I've been thinking about it and you're quite an okay person, really.'

'Wow. Thanks,' I muttered.

'No, really,' he persisted. 'Something that our crazy ... I mean, our *counsellor* said actually got me thinking. She said we should try focusing on the most positive memories we have of each other. So I was thinking about that time back in Bangalore, at the airport, when that guy was hassling me about my smoking, how you came and defended me by shouting at him. I remember when I saw you rushing up to us and I felt so happy, thinking, "Here comes my Jhansi ki Rani. Now this guy's had it." Remember that?'

I had no recollection whatsoever of this incident and was privately cursing myself for ever defending his smoking, but out loud I said, 'Wonderful, wonderful. Even the best memory you have of me involves my yelling. That's great. It makes me feel all warm inside.'

'So,' he said, 'what was the incident about me that came to your mind?'

'Well,' I admitted. 'There were a lot. Mostly how you took care of me when I was pregnant. It almost makes me want to get pregnant again.'

He stopped walking and stood there, staring at me.

'Almost,' I clarified.

We started walking again. I continued, 'But seriously. It's just been really hard for me to understand why you suddenly became so cold and unwilling to open up and talk of late ...

I thought we'd always had these problems but things just got so much worse ...'

He looked as if he was struggling with whatever he was planning to say next. Finally, it came out, 'Actually. The thing is that I didn't know how to tell you – it's just that after you moved back here, I was feeling bad because of all our fighting ...' He paused and then continued reluctantly, '... but then I read an SMS exchange on your phone between you and some guy called Gary. I found it difficult to act the same after that.'

This time, I stopped in my tracks and stared incredulously at him. He stopped too and said, his words coming out in a rush, as if he was getting something heavy off his chest, 'I know that you're going to say I had no business reading your text messages and perhaps I didn't, but that doesn't change the fact that you've been having inappropriate exchanges with someone and even though we might be having problems, that really doesn't mean you start to get overly intimate with some old foreign boyfriend or whoever he may be. But last night, when I thought for a minute that you'd actually done something silly, I realized you're much too important to me and that this thing is something that we can get past. And I don't want to hear about him, I've forgiven you already, so ...'

I spoke slowly, my head spinning, 'Wait just a minute, Vijay. What exactly did you read?'

He said sulkily, 'I don't remember. Something about how he missed you and the days in Bangalore before you got married and how great things had been when you were living together. And ...' he added bitterly, '... he ended by saying "Love you". You never even told me that you had lived with someone else before me. Maybe you didn't feel comfortable about it, but it certainly came as a shock to me.'

All of this was making immense sense to me now.

I said with the same sarcasm that I had resolved two minutes ago to control, 'Yes, honey. Or *maybe* Gary is the name that I've used for your brother's wife *Garima* on my phone.'

There was a heavy silence as Vijay registered what I had just said.

I stood there tapping my feet, closely watching his face, very interested in hearing what he would have to say for himself at this point.

He looked around thoughtfully – up at the sky, out at the sea, down at the ground – everywhere but at my face.

'Ah,' he finally said.

I waited for more.

He took me by the shoulder and, gently steering me towards the house, gave me his most winning smile, one that suggested that nothing had ever been out of place between us. 'Ghar chalein?'

13

The Night Under the Stars

Vijay's parents were due to go back to Jaipur. They insisted that they had had a nice time with us, but we knew that Mummyji was missing her kitchen, her garden and her park waali ladies; and Papaji wanted to go back to his familiar routine too.

Their flight was on Saturday morning at about 9 a.m. and Vijay and I went to drop them off at the airport. We touched their feet in parting and when I straightened up, Mummyji held me by the shoulders and then reached up to hug me. She was clearly feeling emotional and her 'achhe se rehna' was both a blessing and the extraction of a promise from us. They went into the airport while Vijay and I waited outside for a few minutes.

We had offered to get them some sort of assistance inside the airport but Papaji, who never took a favour if he could help it, said they would manage fine. And sure enough, as we watched them a tad anxiously through the glass, they did seem to be finding their bearings and were already heading for the right queue. As we followed their progress with our eyes, I heard Vijay chuckling softly to himself.

When I asked him what was funny, he said, 'Nothing. I just think they make a cute couple.'

I looked at them once more. Papaji, tall and white-haired, carrying their one simple tiny suitcase, with his slow but sure long strides, occasionally stopping to look at his boarding pass to check some detail – and Mummyji in her pink sari, the pallu over her head, a whole head shorter than Papaji, taking quick steps in her small flat sandals to keep pace with him. I was surprised to find I had a lump in my throat, which I quickly swallowed. Yes, they actually *were* a rather cute couple.

Married for over fifty years and so in tune with each other that they never even fought. I did the math. Married about *fifteen* times longer than me and Vijay – and no earthquake-related emergency evacuations to their credit, at least none that I was aware of.

'Ladne ki kya baat hain? Kabhi main maan jaati hoon, kabhi wo maan jaate hain.' Mummyji's voice rang in my ears.

She had made it sound so simple.

My god.

Could it really *be* that simple?

That afternoon, I asked Vijay, 'I know having Peanut has been the best possible thing in the world and all that. But do you sometimes miss the days when it was just us?'

Peanut had been really cranky since about noon and we had been taking turns carrying and rocking her for the last two hours. It was only now at about 2 p.m. that she had finally tired herself out and fallen asleep. Being possibly even more tired than her, we were also taking the opportunity to lie down on either side of her.

He replied almost immediately, 'Of course. Especially when we were in Bangalore. The house to ourselves, only part-time help ... when we could cuddle up together on the sofa and watch four hours of *Friends*, uninterrupted ...'

'... when we could just drop everything and drive out of town for the weekends ...' I interjected.

'... and we would drag our blankets up to the roof and sleep under the stars ...'

'Oh my god,' I said, remembering. 'We used to sleep on the roof, under the *stars* ... and the big moon and clouds and watch for shooting stars ...' It all came back in a rush to me and I was overcome by a deep sense of nostalgia. 'It seems so long ago ... everything is different now ... Are those days gone forever?'

'No,' Vijay assured me. 'Only for the next eighteen years – then Peanut will get out of the house and hopefully take Kajal with her and it will be just you and me again.'

'Great,' I muttered. I thought for a while and said with a touch of wistfulness, 'I think I miss sleeping under the stars most. I don't think I've even *seen* a sky full of stars for years now.'

Vijay only listened quietly. I guessed he was lost in the reminiscing.

At night, it was even tougher trying to put Peanut to bed because I was doing it all by myself and trying to get her used to sleeping in her own room for a change. I first fed her, then lay down with her and read her three bedtime stories, the pictures of which she looked at with great interest. I sang her two lullabies and tickled her tummy lightly until she drifted off. With this cleverly devised, well-thought-out and ridiculously elaborate bedtime routine, she was finally asleep by 11.45 p.m. I kissed her soft white cheeks, quietly tucked her light blanket around her and went back into our room.

Tonight, Vijay had not helped me with Peanut's routine at all and this made me feel a bit annoyed. He had kept calling out that he was busy whenever I asked him to come in. I presumed that he had probably been Facebooking again. I finally walked into our room to see him sitting on the bed and just as I was about to tell him off, I noticed he was giving me a strange sort of look.

'Why are you looking at me like that?' I asked suspiciously.

'Like what?' he said.

'I don't know ... All ... cockeyed.'

'Cockeyed?' he said indignantly. 'Honey, that's my special romantic look. You forgot?'

'Oh,' I said. 'I guess it's been a *really* long time. But anyway, I don't feel romantic. How can I, after putting our baby to bed for about three hours – all by *myself*.' I flopped onto the bed, exhausted.

He wriggled over to me and said, 'Well, maybe this will change your mood.' And he switched off the light.

The room was flooded with darkness and I found I was looking up at a sky full of stars and a beautiful crescent moon.

Vijay had covered half the ceiling right above our bed with glow-in-the-dark stickers. The twinkling stars and the bright crescent moon on the black ceiling gave the eerie yet romantic effect of a night sky – if not a real night sky, at least a planetarium-type night sky. I stared up at it in utter delight and noted that he had thoughtfully arranged seven of the stars into the Big Dipper. It was slightly awry, but it immediately caught my fancy and became my favourite part of the effort.

'It's beautiful,' I said.

'You like it?' I knew he was beaming, even though I couldn't see his face.

'Love it,' I said. 'It's brilliant.'

He stretched his arm out invitingly and I lay my head on his shoulder and curled up against him, still looking at the night sky he had created for us. We were both quiet for a few moments. His breathing was steady and calm in my ear and I murmured seductively to him, 'It's not exactly the same as the Bangalore night sky. But it's definitely kind of romantic, isn't it?'

I was answered by a gentle snore.

I smiled to myself in the darkness and wrapped one arm and one leg tight around my sleeping husband. He stirred a bit and murmured something into my hair that sounded suspiciously like 'Goodnight … my little Buntvinder,' and then his breathing became even once more as he drifted off.

I lay there with a silly smile pasted on my face and a feeling of unusual satisfaction spreading warmly through my entire body. Maybe things hadn't changed that much after all.

Besides, we'd only had three years together. There was clearly a long, bumpy road ahead of us, stretching maybe – who knew – about fifty years?

Which, I thought as I finally drifted off, was just fine by me.

Acknowledgements

I owe a lot to the following people, so a big thank you to:

My grandmother Didu, who told me that 'to have a talent like writing and not use it is a Sin Against God.' Dear me.

My mother Chitra, sister Gitanjali and my best friends Richa Srivastava and Kunal Ganju — who read, believed in and critiqued various versions of the story.

The people who helped me through the maze of first-time publishing — Vivek Gaur, for all his help and advice about getting started and my aunt, Poonam Sahi, who guided me at every step in a very fairy godmother-like manner.

The team at HarperCollins — especially Karthika VK, who apparently startled her driver by laughing out loud while reading the manuscript in her car and Resham George, for her gentle yet firm deletions of extra material and overall painstaking work. Shantanu Ray Chaudhuri, for running his eagle eye over the book to put all the finishing touches it needed. Also, Saurav for the design and Shuka Jain for the art direction on the cover — and for being eminently good-humoured and tolerant about my nit-picking.

The rest of the family for all their support, especially Vijay's parents, who also became mine — Mummyji and Papaji.

And last but not least, Vijay himself — the ever-patient, ever-forgiving, constant source of material that I call my husband. Honey, you're a lot of things, but above all, you're a riot.

Also by Yashodhara Lal

Sorting Out Sid

An Extract

The Script Presentation

Sid tapped his fingers on the table for a while in a pensive mood. Finally, the door swung open and Ravi ushered in the agency team along with a couple of other brand managers. The first person to enter was Murali, the head of the agency. He burst in with his usual boisterous confidence and flourishing moustache, booming, 'How are you, Sid?' and extended his hand.

'Fine, FINE,' said Sid in a loud and deep voice that came pretty close to matching Murali's in terms of pitch, allowing his hand to be pumped in Murali's death grip. They had never really liked each other. Sid thought Murali was a condescending gasbag, and he had always felt Murali resented dealing with a client so much younger than himself. They stood there smiling affably at one another. 'Take a seat, Murali, so good to see you. Coffee?'

'Sure, would love one,' said Murali, and plonked himself heavily on one of the chairs as the rest of his team piled in. Sid greeted each one and noted with a heavy heart that it was a crowd today – about ten people? His heart sank. This was bad news; he knew this only happened when there was a particularly horrendous script idea, and thus the need for reinforcements. Right now in the room, Sid noted, were people from the servicing team, the copy team, the creative head, the account director and one small fellow whom Sid hadn't seen before, and vaguely suspected to be the office tea boy. Still, one would hear them out – one hardly had a choice.

Once everyone had settled down and the pleasantries about the weather were out of the way, Sid cleared his throat and said, 'So, can we start?'

Murali opened his mouth to speak, but Ravi piped in, 'Sid, Akash said he would join us, should we wait for him?' Sid gave Ravi a withering look which had absolutely no impact on the young man. He was about to say that there was no need to wait, and that Akash would pick up the threads, when the door opened and Akash came in, bustling with self-importance. Murali stood up to greet Akash as did the rest of the agency. Sid cringed inwardly. Whenever Murali and Akash met, the conversation between them was always extended and jovial, with entirely senseless rambling. It was to be no different this time. After ten minutes more of poor jokes, meaningless reminiscing and comments about the weather, a lull in the conversation indicated it was finally time to start the script presentation. Sid looked at his watch – 11.30 a.m., already! And not one useful task had yet been accomplished all morning.

Murali put on his serious business face and turned to Akash. 'Akash, we have something brilliant for you today, you're going to love it. It's brilliant, boss! When you hear it, you're going to say, "brilliant!".' Akash nodded as if under a spell, but Murali continued with a warning in his tone, 'But, you have to be able to see it, you have to be able to visualize … and if you can't visualize it…' He shook his head sorrowfully. '… you won't be able to appreciate it.'

Akash nodded sagely and Sid cleared his throat, irritated that Murali seemed to be addressing only Akash. Murali continued, 'Rimi came up with this script, so, I'd like her to present. Go ahead, Rimi.'

Sid noted that Akash had assumed his listening stance – he leaned back on his chair with a serious expression and covered his eyes with his hand. Rimi looked confused but Murali indicated that she should go ahead.

Rimi was a thin, pale young girl with long, flowing, black hair who had always given Sid the impression of being an anorexic ghost who smoked too much. She took a deep breath, closed her eyes and started narrating the script in a low monotone that she presumably thought was very captivating and sexy.

'The story opens with the camera panning out over a modern-looking room. There is a row of four beds, each of which has one person fast asleep under the covers. We cannot see who they are until suddenly there is a ray of sunshine that beams through the window over each of the beds in quick succession. As this happens, the people on the bed throw off their bed covers in perfect synchronization. As they emerge, we see that they are four very beautiful, young girls. They stretch in synchronization and step out of their beds in synchronization. In perfect synchronization they get ready quickly and have their breakfast. They step out of the house in synchronized steps. We then see that they have reached another building. At this building, they step inside and go into a changing room where there are four empty booths waiting for them. In perfect synchronization, they step into the changing booths and when they step out we see they are in swimming suits. In the climax of the film, all four dive in perfect synchronization into a swimming pool and it is revealed to us that they are in fact – synchronized swimmers!'

There were a few long moments of silence – of anticipation on the agency's side, horror on Sid's part. Akash was nodding slowly, his hand still covering his eyes.

As per protocol, Akash, as the most senior person, was supposed to speak first. Everyone waited … and waited. Finally, Akash uncovered his eyes and spoke, but only to sidestep smoothly by saying, 'I'm still absorbing it. Sid, you want to react first?'

This was exactly what Sid had been hoping for. Biting back sarcasm, he asked politely, 'This is supposed to be an ad for our lead toilet cleaner, Kollinex. I must have missed the part where that came in?'

Rimi fumbled with her script, the very picture of ghostly, pale confusion, but Murali stepped in, booming, 'Well, obviously Rimi didn't spell it out, Sid, but the very idea here is to bring a certain glamour to the category. These girls are well rested and fresh in the morning. "Fresh in the morning". The morning routine consists of bathroom visits – it's about the concept. Here we are trying to give you a feel of the whole story without the boring product windows and brand specifics.' He paused for impact, and to give Sid a look that magnificently combined superiority with reproach. 'But of course, you have to be able to visualize it.'

Work Sid prided himself on being a cool character whose feathers rarely got ruffled. Right now, however, he felt the blood rushing to his ears. He was on the verge of telling Murali to visualize exactly where he could stuff his lousy script, when Akash finally cleared his throat and looked up at the several tense faces around the room.

He exclaimed, 'I can see it! I can visualize!'

As Sid looked on in dumbstruck horror, unable to believe his ears, Akash continued, 'Apart from the minor point that

Sid has mentioned, I think this is indeed brilliant!' The agency faces lit up with happy, relieved smiles as he continued, 'It is attention grabbing! It has glamour! It has a story! Brilliant! Let's create the storyboard and put it into research quickly!'

He got up to shake Murali's hand. The meeting was concluded amidst happy laughter and jubilation all around. Sid sat glued to his chair, numb with shock. His team looked confused and disappointed, with one notable exception – young, enthusiastic Ravi who continued to take what appeared to be copious notes, pausing every now and then to shoot gleeful looks around the room.

The agency left shortly thereafter. Sid presumed they planned to take the rest of the day off getting drunk. He bade them farewell, his fake work-smile pasted on his face. The room emptied and Sid was the last to leave. He sighed as he went back to his desk with heavy steps, and a thought entered his mind – would it be premature to resign before finding alternative employment?

8

Sid and Brownie

Sid lay sprawled on his favourite beanbag, legs spread out wide, clutching a bottle of Kingfisher. The beer was ice cold – he could feel it through his shirt against his belly. He had four more bottles on the floor, within arm's reach of him. He did not intend to get up from his beanbag, not even for a smoke. He knew the beer would warm up as the evening progressed and so he had set the air conditioner at 17 degrees. Of course, at 17 degrees he would want to pee more than usual. But he had emptied his bladder just before settling down and that would help take care of the urge for a while. Sometimes you just had to prepare yourself and hope for the best.

He took another sip of beer, savouring it as it ran down his throat, sloshing about a bit before settling down in his empty stomach. No dinner tonight. Dinner arguments had been the worst of late. But tonight Mandira was out for an office party and he was home alone with no need for the formality of dinner. Home alone! Just the way he liked it. He lovingly patted his beanbag, which he fondly called Brownie when no one else was around.

Mandira never seemed to understand why Sid valued his time alone so much. Being alone meant no pressure to perform or pretend, no need to be funny and entertain the crowd. He had never been able to explain it to her properly. He knew his natural tendency to perform was the reason she noticed him in college, choosing to go out with him even though she was a much-in-demand senior. But then, after their marriage, even when it was just the two of them, she seemed to expect that he would continue to be the official entertainer. She didn't understand who this quiet person was – the one who just wanted to spend hours reading or listening to music or watching TV. She had been dismayed, and even considered it some kind of personal rejection.

'Why is it that you have a hundred stories to tell other people, but you can't even tell me about your day at work?' had been her pet peeve.

He had attempted to tell her that this quiet side of him was also a part of who he was, especially when people weren't around. But she continued to take it as a sign of his diminishing interest in her. For a while he tried hard to be attentive and amusing while she was around, but it had been a constant strain. It made him crankier than usual, eventually leading to the same thing he had been trying to avoid – squabbling.

He took another sip, this time glugging it down long and slow. Constant strain was perhaps marginally better than explosive attacks like the one that had happened today.

Mandira was hysterical when she had called him at the office. For some strange reason she had been going through his personal laptop at home when she discovered his private collection of porn – one that Sid had carefully built over the last few years. His collection was impressive and extensive, in both volume and variety. The discovery enraged her although Sid didn't quite understand why. A man had needs, and she sure as hell hadn't been fulfilling them for a long time now. In fact, of late, she had even taken to sleeping in the guestroom – ostensibly, his reading light disturbed her. Sid, however, was certain that he heard her talking on the phone late into the night. So it was, apparently, only a means to avoid him. What was a guy to do? Porn was only a little, innocent voyeurism. It helped in getting him some sort of … well, release. She was the one who said he bottled things up too much and that wasn't healthy. Talk about double standards, he thought moodily.

She had screamed at him on the phone for his perverted nature, how it now made a lot of sense that he no longer expressed any interest in any physical contact with her. And how sneaky it was of him to hide this sick side from her. It had all been a bit too much for him and he tried to argue with her, in a low whispered tone, mindful of the many people around in the office. 'Me not expressing interest … And you're calling me sneaky? What were you doing going through my personal stuff, anyway? It clearly shows that you don't trust me.'

Mandira had stopped fuming and hyperventilating to give Sid a short bark of a laugh and said, 'You've got to be kidding me, Siddharth. Do you really think that's the main issue at hand?' Sid hesitated for a moment and she continued, 'And anyway – you've shown you aren't worthy of trust!'

Frustrated, Sid whispered that he couldn't talk at the moment and suggested that they discuss it when he got home. Her voice changed abruptly, and became all cold. She informed him that she was leaving for an office party and would get back late. She added somewhat unnecessarily, in his opinion, that he could entertain himself with his Cowgirl-in-High-Heeled-Boots fantasies. Before he could say another word in protest, she slammed the phone down.

'Okay, fine, so we'll talk at home then, honey, see you,' Sid said in a loud and cheerful tone for the benefit of his colleagues who were pretending not to listen. Sid looked around discreetly – he had a lot of experience with reading ears, and he knew immediately all their attention had been focussed on him. He was also aware of his own ears giving him away as they flushed bright red despite his attempt to cover up by shuffling through papers and pursing his lips into a tuneless whistle. A thought sprung into his mind that he might soon get a cabin of his own now that he was slated to become a vice president. It would be useful on days like this.

'Arrey ... Khatam?' Sid looked with surprise and confusion at his empty beer bottle. That was quick. He had intended to savour his first bottle, savour the feeling of an evening alone at home and the ability to do exactly what he wanted. Chalo, no matter, he still had a few bottles to go. He leaned over and stretched out to grab another bottle, singing out an impromptu and cheerful ditty.

'Come here, my dear, you are so near…

Please have no fear, I love my beer…'

He ransacked his brain to come up with a last line that would do justice to the poet in him. But he could only manage a lame 'And my name is … Sid'. He cackled at his own silliness. He had been going for the style of Urdu poets, like Ghalib. The last line of a couplet usually had the writer's name inserted into it, as a sort of signature. It didn't always work, he decided. Those Urdu poet guys weren't practical, he concluded. No wonder most of them were dead. Still, they had churned out some pretty riveting stuff. Sid liked Urdu couplets and felt the urge to recite one, but for the life of him he couldn't remember a single one at the moment.

He used his handy-dandy Swiss pocket-knife-cum-bottle-opener-cum-keychain to pop the cap off the second beer bottle and took another long, cold swig. He let out a loud 'aaaah…' as he leaned back and closed his eyes. He tended to get vocal when he got high irrespective of whether he had an audience or not. He just felt the need to speak, and it was nice to be able to speak without being judged.

He felt a fart coming, but held it in. He wasn't going to fart on his favourite beanbag. It wouldn't be fair to her. He patted her lovingly. It felt natural to converse with her at the moment. 'Eh, Brownie? What has it been, fifteen years? We've been through too much for me to fart on you, right?' Fifteen years with Mandira too, but wouldn't mind farting on her right now, he thought, and immediately regretted it. That was low, below the belt, you might say. He giggled.

He shifted around a bit, snuggling deeper into Brownie. She was undoubtedly his favourite piece of furniture. She was one of the first purchases Mandira and he had made together. Well, he had made the purchase; Mandira had protested vociferously that a dirty brown beanbag wouldn't go with anything else that she had in mind for the house. Sid let Mandira have her way on most counts, but on this one, he had put his foot down and insisted that he was buying the beanbag; he needed one to relax on, and besides, he insisted, it wasn't dirty brown, it was chocolatey, really. Finally, she yielded, though grudgingly, and they had carted Brownie home. However, he had since caught her many times giving Brownie glares that alternated between merely disdainful to positively malevolent. Sid defiantly resisted all her attempts – and there had been quite a few over the years – to get rid of Brownie. During every furniture rearrangement, Mandira tried to convince Sid that Brownie was now too old and tatty in contrast to the rest of the furniture in the living room. To this, Sid would always say that Brownie was getting more and more comfortable with the passing years. In fact, Sid once claimed that when he died, he wanted to be buried with Brownie.

'You're not Christian, Sid – you will be cremated and not buried.'

'Whatever. I want Brownie with me.'

Sorting Out Sid

Meet Sid, a master at the art of denial, in this hilarious, insightful tale of modern-day living and relationships, Siddharth Agarwal a.k.a. Sid has it all – a fifteen-year-long marriage, a bunch of devoted friends, and the chance to be the company's youngest-ever VP, all at the age of thirty-six.

But, behind the scenes, his life is slowly falling apart, what with his marriage on the rocks, parents who treat him like a delinquent child, and overly interfering, backstabbing friends. And that's not even counting the manipulative HR vixen and the obnoxious boss he must tackle in office.

So, when lovely, spunky single mom Neha materializes in his life, she brings into it a ray of hope. But will she cause the brewing storm to finally erupt?

Who said it would be easy sorting out Sid?

Coming Soon: Dear Rimi

Fiercely independent Rimi Ahluwalia, 28, doesn't need anyone in her life. She's content with her climb up the corporate ladder at a media company in fast-moving Mumbai. Until she is fired.

Now Rimi is faced with the challenge of having to take care of her aged and eccentric parents on rapidly dwindling finances and poor job prospects. Desperate, she takes up an assignment – as the new Agony Aunt – for the lead publication with the same company that fired her in the first place. Before she knows it, the column takes off and becomes famous. Except nobody knows it's her, apart from the super-bitchy editorial staff she has to deal with.

And then he arrives in her life, Sahil of the so-called 'psychic powers'. Between her new assignment, her parents, a best friend who's driving her up the wall and this strange new man, Rimi's life is turning upside down. Will she succumb to the persuasions of money and love, or is there a way out of the chaos?

Look out for Yashodhara Lal's next novel *Dear Rimi* to find out!